The Wild Palate

D0879554

Recent books by Walter Hall

Nonfiction:
Barnacle Parp's Chain Saw Guide,
Rodale Press, 1977

Poems:
Miners Getting Off the Graveyard,
Burning Deck Press, 1978

The WILD PALATE

A serious wild foods cookbook

Walter and Nancy Hall

Illustrations by David Frampton
Designed by Joan Peckolick

Rodale Press, Emmaus, Pennsylvania

Printed in the United States of America on recycled paper, containing a high percentage of de-inked fiber.

Library of Congress Cataloging in Publication Data

Hall, Walter, 1940–
    The wild palate, a serious wild foods cookbook.

    Includes index.
    1. Cookery (Wild foods)   2. Wild plants, Edible—North America.   3. Food, Wild—North America.
I. Hall, Nancy, joint author.   II. Title.
TX823.H27   641.5   80-12530
ISBN 0-87857-303-8 hardcover
ISBN 0-87857-302-X paperback

2 4 6 8 10 9 7 5 3 1 hardcover
2 4 6 8 10 9 7 5 3 1 paperback

for
Roger Yepsen

CONTENTS

PREFACE

Barnacle Parp leaned on the tree that was leaning on his new chain saw. He chuckled as the grasshoppers and angry flickers quieted. Then he walked from the fir into the sage and down the hill to the stream. He looked into a deep pool between boulders, pulled off his sawdust, rubbed his eyes, and jumped. Life scattered outward in ripples and vapors, along with Parp's sweaty chips and itches.

Parp's hasty clamber up the opposite bank cost him a scraped belly on an unseen rock. He crawled to a grassy spot and lay in the late sun to dry. Behind him, high on a slide, three marmots whistled in turn. A single eagle planed from the horizon and dipped out of sight. Dusk whispered of peace even in the midst of hectic summer. He looked to the altered future with a smile.

Parp's memory wandered back over his mountain life—the long winters and crazy summers in which he had learned his ways. Since he would not be gathering wood this summer, he thought perhaps he'd pull together his notes and files and see if that long-dreamed-of cookbook could become a reality. He knew a certain writer who might help.

Parp pondered the idea half the night and started working early in the morning. It took his summer and his fall and all the extra time of winter. When summer returned, the project was complete.

blue berries

INTRODUCTION

GATHERING WILD FOODS

This book should be useful to anyone who hunts, fishes, or gathers wild foods in North America. There are many people who enjoy gathering wild foods and there are many levels of involvement in this activity. Each spring, thousands of people go out to collect young shoots of edible wild plants. In summer, the woods are populated with mushroom lovers. In autumn, hunters take to the fields. In each season, nature brings forth some bounty and there are always people who use this opportunity to lower their grocery bills, add nourishment to their meals, and enjoy feeling closer to the natural world.

Acquisition is the first step in enjoying wild foods. This may be as simple as picking wild apples, as strenuous as elk hunting, or as complex as foraging through the seasons of edible plants. Foraging demands knowledge, patience, and experience. It also demands the kind of systematic approach to identification detailed in the many competent field guides and formal floras that are now available. In addition to these rather scientific approaches, there are many entertaining books about wild foods, such as those by Euell Gibbons and Bradford Angier. Parp says that beginning foragers should certainly read these informative books, but competent field work requires familiarity with a formal identification system as well. We hope no one will glance at this book, run to a nearby field, pick some *Asclepias subverticillata*, and come home to prepare Parp's recipe for Cooked Milkweed.

The forager is rewarded according to investment. Picking wild apples costs little time or effort but extending the diet appreciably with wild foods requires that the forager spend the time necessary to "key-out" plants for positive identification. This involves disciplined use of a formal flora or good field guide and conscientious observation over periods of time.

Not everyone who uses this book will wish to become an authority on edible wild plants, but everyone who collects wild foods shares one concern: how to properly care for, process, and prepare the foods they gain from nature. We hope this book will help.

PROPER PREPARATION OF WILD FOODS

Parp says it makes no sense to create a fine salad of nutritious wild leafy vegetables and then cover it with a manufactured dressing loaded with preservatives and polysorbate 60. Condiments using wild ingredients are detailed in Chapter Five of this book. Parp's Wild Chutney is especially suited to wild game dishes such as venison, rabbit, and squirrel.

We avoid certain traditional methods of wild food cooking either because they call for processed ingredients or because they incorporate saturated fats. For instance, many woodspeople compensate for the low moisture and fat content of wild meats by cooking everything with bacon fat, butter, or salt pork. We have replaced these ingredients with unrefined, unsaturated oils. Sugar is replaced by honey or other natural sweeteners. We use whole-grain flours, meals, and grains.

The delicate flavors and textures of wild foods can be damaged or ruined by improper treatment. Many people overcook wild vegetables and meats. Except where noted otherwise, vegetables should be cooked in scant water, just enough to produce steam, and until tender.

Tender portions of wild game normally require far less cooking time than do domestic meats. The wild or gamey taste that people associate with wild foods is often caused by overcooking.

Parp believes in slow cooking and rare meat. There is a real health danger in overcooking meats, especially those prepared quickly on a hot surface or in the flames of a barbecue pit. Those meats that must be thoroughly cooked should be baked, roasted, or simmered in stews and soups.

THE QUALITY OF WILD FOODS

In some areas, the U.S. Forest Service employs the appalling practice of spraying the wilderness with deadly chemicals such as dioxin-containing herbicides such as 2,4,5-T. Spraying is going on in the Pacific Northwest (especially Oregon) and other regions. Unfortunately, there is no guarantee that any particular wilderness will be entirely free of herbicides, pesticides, or industrial pollution. Parp says it shouldn't be that way and thinks all of us who share his conviction should take appropriate action. Chemical contamination is the only real threat from wild foods and that threat is considerably less from the wild than it is from any grocery store. But if you believe that your nearby marsh was sprayed with insecticides last year or the year before, you should gather your cattails elsewhere.

As for natural nutrition, wild foods can't be beat. Wild meat contains more protein, more minerals, less fat, and fewer calories than domestic meat. Wild vegetables are likewise more nutritious than domestic varieties and wild fruits are so superior that there is no comparison. If you use wild herbs, spices, and vegetables, or organically grown ones, and if you take reasonable care in your selection, preservation, and preparation of wild food, you will enjoy the most healthful and delicious meals possible.

PRESERVING WILD FOODS

Freezing is no doubt the fastest, easiest, safest, and most common method of preserving wild foods. But it is not the cheapest, and many who will use this book have chosen to live beyond the reach of the utility companies and so have no place to plug in a freezer.

The traditional methods of preserving food are canning, jerking, and drying. For a comprehensive guide to these and other methods of preserving, we recommend *Stocking Up* (Rodale Press, 1978). Below are a few additional notes which may be useful.

Freezing game meat

All meats can be frozen, including edible organ meats such as heart, brains, and liver. You may also freeze soups and stews made from the less meaty portions of animals, as well as scraps and suet. These last are useful as pet food, as food for wild birds and animals, and as fat to be ground with meat for hamburger. If you plan on preserving and using all of these items, there will be very little waste.

Any wild game larger than rabbit will benefit from hanging before freezing, unless you can get your meat into the freezer immediately after the body heat has cooled away. In all cases, allow meat to cool naturally before placing it in the freezer.

The rugged terrain of the Rocky Mountains affects our approach to this problem. We usually hunt in very high country that is accessible only on foot. This means, of course, that we must carry out our meat in backpacks. Since only two or three of us go at a time, we can't plan on carrying a whole elk home in one trip. We usually stuff our packs full of plastic bags containing the heart, liver, tongue, hide, and whatever else we can carry, then cover the rest of the carcass with spruce boughs. Then we make as many return trips as necessary to retrieve the rest of the meat. This means that most of the meat cools naturally for several days in fresh high-mountain air or in a snowbank. We freeze the meat immediately after arriving home with each load. That way our freezer doesn't strain to freeze an entire elk carcass all at once.

One thing to remember is that freezing is itself a tenderizing process. It is much slower than hanging, but if your game is in the freezer for six months or more, you won't be able to tell whether it was hung or not.

Use your freezer most efficiently by freezing only the meatiest portions of small game and fowl, including the backs and hind quarters of small animals and the breasts of such birds as quail and ptarmigan.

The remaining portions don't have to be wasted. Though American hunters habitually discard them, tough and scrawny pieces make wonderful stock for soups and stews. Some of the world's finest cooking is based on such stocks. Freeze your stock, soups, and stews and they will keep for long periods.

Always remove or trim away the wounded portion of game before freezing. Meat affected by a gunshot wound, even a small one, turns rancid quickly and in any case is not appetizing. You should also trim away the fat from all meats except venison and cut off any areas that are dirty or bruised. Though you should never wash the meat of game birds, red meat may be rinsed in cold water, if necessary, and then washed with vinegar.

Remember that all wild meats dry more rapidly than domestic meats and must be protected against drying and freezer burn. Double-wrap all meat in strong freezer paper and make your wrappings as airtight as possible. Seasoning meat before freezing causes it to absorb oxygen and shortens its freezer life. If you make sausage, season it after thawing rather than before freezing.

Be sure to label and date clearly all wild foods going into your freezer. Use the packages by date, oldest first.

Freezing wild fruits and vegetables

We've found that the least treatment or processing is the best. We wash wild fruit and berries, package them in airtight plastic bags, and freeze immediately. Larger fruits can be sliced and then frozen in bags. Many people rinse sliced fruit in vinegar or lemon juice to preserve the color, but we prefer to lose the color and retain the natural flavor. We simply wash, slice, bag, and freeze, and this process works very well for us. Frozen wild fruit may be used directly from the freezer in any of the recipes in this book.

Except for leafy wild vegetables, you should steam-scald all wild vegetables before freezing. Boil about two inches of water in a large saucepan or steamer. Use a rack and colander to keep vegetables out of the water. Scald wild vegetables in steam for five minutes, then immerse in very cold water for three minutes. Pack in commercial vegetable boxes or plastic bags and freeze immediately with no added spices or sweeteners.

Canning

Canning is an excellent preserving method for those of us who live beyond the last utility pole or do not have freezers. Before electricity brought the freezer into many homes, canning was the most common method of preserving fruits, vegetables, and meats. It is still widely used in rural areas where power shortages or surges are common.

Again, *Stocking Up* is an excellent guide to safe canning and we recommend that anyone attempting canning for the first time should consult this book or another detailed guide to the subject. We offer here a few notes especially for wild foods gatherers.

Small game. To can small game, process it as soon as the body heat is gone. Completely remove all fat and omit seasoning. Do not attempt to process any small game meat that is bloodshot and contaminated, or that is not perfectly fresh and wholesome.

To prepare small game for canning, completely remove all skin, fat, and bones. Cut into small pieces and simmer the meat in stock until it is medium done and tender. Use a standard hot-pack canning process with a pressure canner. Place the boned meat into quart jars with at least 1½ inches of headspace. Cover the meat with stock, seal the jars, and process in the canner at ten pounds of pressure for 90 minutes. Use these directions to can any wildfowl.

Big game. Again, meat to be canned must be uncontaminated by gunshot, dirt, leaves, or hair. If any of these have affected the meat, either discard it, or clean it thoroughly and cook immediately. Do not attempt to can it.

Good cuts of meat are best for canning because they will retain the highest quality. Cut the best meat into strips just a little shorter than the jars you'll be using. Cut with the grain of the meat, lengthwise. Cook the strips above scant water until medium done. Do not season or salt. Pack in quart canning jars and allow adequate headspace. Cover with boiling stock and process at ten pounds of pressure for two hours.

Open-air jerking

Freezing and canning are excellent, healthful methods for preserving wild foods, but they are moderately technical and obviously require proper equipment. Curing and smoking will not be described in this book because both methods involve chemicals or processes known to be unsafe. Here is Parp's favorite way of preserving meat—a method as old as the sun.

In the high meadows of the San Juan Mountains the intense sun and cool, clean air are perfect for open-air jerking. Although not all areas are blessed with this perfect combination, meat can be safely jerked in any area where the sun shines and the humidity and pollution aren't excessive.

Here's how we do it. As soon as the season opens, we form a hunting party and make our way to the high country. Each person carries a hunting license and rifle. We cross the high meadows that stretch on for miles until finally we make camp in the trees below a certain ridge. Then we begin to hunt.

As each person fills a license, the animal is gutted, cleaned, and spread to cool. Each night we feast on elk heart, liver, or tongue. Hides are salted and rolled to be tanned in the easy months of winter.

The meat of an elk is very heavy and a high percentage of that weight is water. Sun jerking removes most of the water, thus reducing the weight by as much as 80 percent. Most of the nutrients and proteins are retained and no harmful chemicals or processes are used.

Each morning, those who are not hunting set to work on the unprocessed meat hidden in caches all around camp. We remove our clothes to avoid staining them with blood, and to soak up that sun. We cut all the meat into thin strips about an inch wide, an inch thick, and up to 12 inches long. We take great care to keep the strips clean and to be sure all hairs are removed.

As we cut, we hang the strips over thin ropes that are strung in a grid pattern in a small meadow near camp. The little meadow is close enough to camp to keep unwelcome guests away and is just open enough to receive full sun. We hang the strips of meat in sequence so we can keep track of the jerking time. After 48 hours the strips are done. They are then stored and used in soups, stews, sandwiches, or eaten plain. They are tender and delicious, completely safe and wholesome, and as natural as any meat could ever be. You can even taste the sun.

WILD SEASONINGS

Whenever possible, Parp prefers to replace domestic seasonings with wild substitutes. Many of the recipes in this book call for wild seasonings which are quite widespread and easy to accumulate, although such accumulation often requires an investment of time and effort. The effort is worthwhile, though, for these wild seasonings are usually more healthful and nutritious than domestic ingredients.

Any ingredient may be classed as a seasoning if it is included with other foods primarily for its flavor rather

than for its nutritional qualities. Many of the wild foods
described in this book have some use as seasoning or as
flavoring in cooked dishes. These uses are frequently
mentioned elsewhere in passing. Here follow Parp's
notes on the wild substances he considers essential
seasonings.

Coltsfoot. *Tussilago* spp.

Coltsfoot ash is a fine substitute for salt. Make it from
fairly mature green leaves in mid-summer. Roll the
leaves into balls in the palms of your hands, using a
little water if necessary. Then place the balled leaves in
the sun, preferably on a hot rock, and allow them to dry
thoroughly. When they are dry, place the balls in a dry
skillet over very high heat. Crush the large chunks that
form and store them in a glass container. Use the ash as
a salt substitute in any recipe, in about the same
amounts as you would use salt, or a little less according
to taste.

Cow parsnip (cow cabbage). *Heracleum lanatum*

Although some people eat the entire plant, cow parsnip
is not a very palatable green. Its best role is as a
seasoning. The leaves, burned and crushed like coltsfoot, may be sprinkled over foods. A slice of stem from
low on the cow parsnip is unbeatable as a salt substitute in stews, soups, roasts, and similarly cooked
dishes.

Peppergrass (mustard bite). *Lepidium fremontii*

This plant goes almost unmentioned in either modern
or ancient herbal literature and was apparently un-

known in the Old World. In our area it is known only to a few members of the Ute and Cheyenne tribes and does not even appear in most field guides or academic studies. Yet it is potentially one of the most useful plants, especially for all of us who are hopelessly addicted to a pungent, peppery taste. Peppergrass seeds can be gathered in great quantity and stored for long periods. Use them in place of ground black pepper, or combine with mild vinegar and coltsfoot ash to make a versatile dressing for meats and sandwiches.

Spicebush. *Lindera benzoin*

Spicebush is a very common shrub with aromatic leaves, stems, and berries that can be steeped for tea. You can dry the berries in the sun, then grind or pound them into a fine powder and use in place of allspice, or as a seasoning in almost any dish where a spicy herbal taste is desired.

Sweet cicely (sweetroot). *Osmorhiza obtusa*

Sweet cicely has a sweet, aniselike flavor, which makes it a fine ingredient for baked goods, wild brews, and vegetable drinks. To prepare the roots for flavoring, dry them thoroughly, then grate into thin strips. Store the strips in corked spice bottles away from sunlight. For this purpose, sweet cicely roots may be dug at any time of the year.

Wild ginger (ginger). *Asarum* spp.

All species of wild ginger have roots that may be prepared for use as a spice. To do so, scrape the roots thoroughly, then place in boiling water to cover. If the plant is in blossom, add the flowers as well to increase the ginger flavor. Boil until the water is half-gone, then place the solution in direct sunlight. When all the liquid has evaporated, grind or pound the solids into a fine powder. Use as ginger in any recipe.

Wild mint. *Mentha* spp.

The aroma and flavor of mint are well known everywhere, and one species of mint or another grows wild in all regions of North America. At one time, mint was used extensively to flavor stews, soups, sauces, salads, and roasts. It is an excellent seasoning. Gather young leaves, dry them, and store in airtight glass containers. We suggest that you experiment boldly with mint as a seasoning for all sorts of foods.

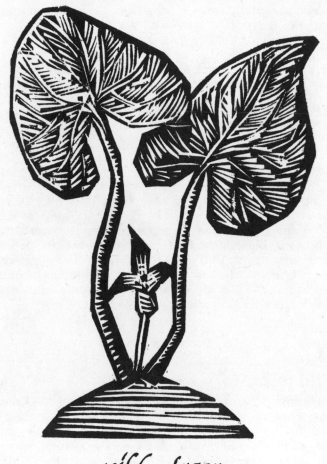

wild ginger

INGREDIENTS AND SUBSTITUTES

Most of the ingredients specified in these recipes are actually wild substitutes for common, domestic ingredients. Parp realizes that not everyone will have access to all these ingredients, or even most of them. Therefore, the following table of possible substitutes will no doubt be useful to many cooks.

Ingredient	*Substitute*
bulrush shoots	green beans, asparagus
caraway root	carrot or similar root
cattail shoots	green beans, asparagus
coconut milk	skim milk
coltsfoot ash	salt, lemon juice
daylily flowers and buds (as thickener)	arrowroot or cornstarch
ground cherries	tomatoes
Indian potatoes	domestic potatoes (quartered) or other tubers
liverberries	diced chicken or duck giblets
manna grass seed	caraway seed
milkweed shoots	green beans
peppergrass seed	ground black pepper
spicebush	allspice
violet leaves and buds (as thickener)	arrowroot or cornstarch
wild mustard or wild mustard powder	domestic mustard
wild rice flour	rye or wheat flour

CHAPTER ONE

WILD APPETIZERS

Wild edibles may be used to concoct all manner of appetizers, ranging from effective to wonderful. Effective wild appetizers will force you to eat something else just to get the taste out of your mouth. Wonderful wild appetizers, on the other hand, may taste so good that you'll never get to the rest of the meal. Elk Heart Spread, for example, will hold a party at the hors d'oeuvres until a slow meal is finally prepared. Incidentally, it's wise to sample your wild preparations before serving them to others and, of course, be sure to verify your identification of all wild foods.

WILD APPETIZERS

ARROWHEAD SPREAD

½ cup arrowhead tubers, diced

¼ cup coconut, shredded

1 tablespoon safflower oil

¼ cup yogurt

¼ teaspoon wild mint

Blend arrowhead, coconut, and safflower oil in a blender until smooth. Add more oil if necessary.

Turn mixture into a bowl. Stir in yogurt and mint. Blend well and chill. Serve cold.

WILD CARROT SPREAD

1 cup wild carrots, cut in pieces

1 teaspoon peppergrass seeds

2 tablespoons yogurt

1 tablespoon light honey

¼ teaspoon coltsfoot ash

1 teaspoon safflower oil

Place all ingredients in a blender and blend until smooth. Add more yogurt, if desired.

DANDELION SPREAD

1 cup raw, young dandelion leaves and roots, chopped and torn in very small pieces

½ cup yogurt

¼ cup hazelnuts or chestnuts, chopped very fine

1 tablespoon plantain leaf, torn in small pieces

3 tablespoons safflower oil

Combine all ingredients in a bowl. Stir to blend well. Chill.

WATERCRESS SPREAD

¼ cup fresh watercress, shredded

⅓ cup wild onions, grated

¼ cup fireweed (*or* other) sprouts

½ cup ground cherries

3 tablespoons Wild French Dressing (page 69)

Place all ingredients except dressing in a blender and blend until smooth.

Turn mixture into a bowl. Stir in Wild French Dressing and blend well. Chill slightly.

SMALL-GAME LIVER SPREAD

- 1 tablespoon olive oil
- ½ pound combined small-game livers, diced (¼ pound rabbit liver, ¼ pound fowl liver)
- ⅓ cup salsify root, scraped and chopped
- ⅓ cup wild carrots, diced
- ⅓ cup wild onions, chopped
- 1 tablespoon safflower oil
- 2 tablespoons yogurt
- ¼ teaspoon wild rosemary
- ¼ teaspoon wild thyme
- ½ teaspoon coltsfoot ash
- 3 tablespoons Wild Vegetable Stock (page 77)

Heat olive oil in a skillet. Sauté liver until lightly browned.

Place liver and all remaining ingredients in a blender. Blend to a smooth spread, adding more stock as needed. Chill before serving.

WILD GOOSE PÂTÉ

Chicken liver may be combined with wild goose liver to create a superb pâté. One hunter rarely has enough goose liver for this recipe. Most pâté recipes are more complex than the one Parp offers here, but we assure you the results will compare favorably with pâtés made by the most difficult Continental methods.

¼ cup game bird drippings (fat from top of refrigerated Wildfowl Stock, page 74)

5 ½-inch slices of goose liver

5 ½-inch slices of chicken liver

4 eggs, boiled almost hard, chopped

½ cup wild onions, chopped

1 teaspoon coltsfoot ash

½ teaspoon peppergrass seeds

¼ teaspoon wild ginger

¼ teaspoon spicebush

Heat ½ of the game bird drippings in a casserole dish.

Sauté liver slices in hot drippings. Turn only once and cook for 8 minutes or less.

Over low heat, combine the eggs with the liver and blend thoroughly with a fork.

Add all remaining ingredients except leftover drippings. Use these drippings, if necessary, to correct the consistency.

Correct seasoning. Place casserole under medium broiler for 7 minutes. Serve hot or cold.

CURRY DIP FOR RAW WILD VEGETABLES

1½ cups yogurt

1 teaspoon peppergrass seeds

1 teaspoon young leaves of broad-leaf plantain, shredded

1 teaspoon young milkweed shoots and greens, chopped

2 tablespoons wild rice flour (*or* 1 tablespoon acorn meal)

½ teaspoon violet flowers and buds, chopped

1½ teaspoons curry powder

Place all ingredients in a blender. Blend at low speed until smooth but not runny. Cover and refrigerate 2 hours or more.

Place dip in a serving dish, surrounded by a variety of raw wild vegetables.

PLANTAIN CRACKERS

2 dozen fresh young plantain leaves

1 egg

½ cup milk

¼ cup cracker crumbs

¼ cup safflower oil

Clean plantain leaves and remove stems.

To make batter, combine egg and milk and beat well. Stir in cracker crumbs.

Heat safflower oil in a small skillet. Dip plantain leaves in batter and sauté in hot oil until fairly crisp. Drain on paper towels. Serve hot or cold as crackers.

WILD CHESTNUT APPETIZER

   1 tablespoon safflower oil
   ¼ teaspoon coltsfoot ash
   ½ teaspoon peppergrass seeds
   2 cups chestnuts, boiled and sliced
   ½ cup tamari soy sauce
   ¼ cup sunflower seeds

Combine safflower oil, coltsfoot ash, and peppergrass seeds in a saucepan. Place over low heat and add the chestnuts. Heat through, but do not scorch or boil.

Add tamari soy sauce. Continue cooking over very low heat, stirring frequently, until mixture is almost dry.

Place mixture in individual serving dishes. Top with sunflower seeds and chill at least 2 hours before serving. A fine appetizer to precede a light, wild vegetarian dinner.

WILD APPETIZERS

SMALL-GAME KIDNEY SPREAD

- ¼ pound small-game kidney, cooked
- ⅓ cup wild onions, grated
- 1 teaspoon peppergrass seeds
- ½ teaspoon coltsfoot ash
- ¼ teaspoon wild thyme
- ¼ teaspoon wild sage
- ¼ teaspoon basil
- 1 egg, boiled almost hard
- ½ cup yogurt

Place all ingredients except yogurt in a blender and blend well.

Add yogurt slowly to make a smooth spread. Chill thoroughly before serving.

YAMPA BITS

- 4 cups whole yampa roots
- 2 cups water
- ¼ cup Wild Herb Vinegar (page 68)
- ½ cup honey
- 1 stick cinnamon

Wash the yampa roots and place in a large saucepan. Cover with water and bring to a boil over moderate heat. Reduce heat and simmer, covered, until tender, about 15 or 20 minutes.

Drain yampa and reserve liquid. Remove peels from roots and place roots in a bowl.

Place reserved liquid in saucepan over moderate heat. Add Wild Herb Vinegar, honey, and cinnamon. Bring just to a boil, then pour over yampa roots.

Allow dish to cool about 30 minutes, then cover tightly and refrigerate 12 hours or more. Serve as appetizer or snack.

GROUND CHERRY SPREAD

- 1   cup ground cherries, washed
- 2   tablespoons olive oil
- 2   tablespoons violet flowers and buds
- ½   teaspoon coltsfoot ash
- ¼   teaspoon wild rosemary

Place ground cherries in a small bowl. Cover with olive oil and mash well with a fork.

Add all other ingredients and stir to blend. Chill before serving on chips or crackers.

WILD APPETIZERS

GOOSEBERRY RELISH

   3 cups fresh gooseberries

   ½ cup Wild Applesauce (page 338)

   1 tablespoon lemon juice

   ¼ cup light honey

   ½ teaspoon Wild Herb Vinegar (page 68)

   1 teaspoon juniper berries

Place all ingredients except juniper berries in a blender and blend thoroughly.

Pour into a 1-gallon glass container. Drop in juniper berries. Cover tightly and store 1 week in a cool, dark place.

Remove juniper berries. Place relish in small jars, seal, and store in refrigerator.

AMARANTH SEED APPETIZER

   ¾ cup yogurt

   ¼ cup amaranth seeds

   1 teaspoon violet flowers and buds

   ½ teaspoon coltsfoot ash

   ½ teaspoon wild horseradish, grated

   2 tablespoons young milkweed shoots, chopped very fine

Combine all ingredients and stir to blend well. Serve on crackers.

PICKLED WILD MUSHROOMS

½ cup Wild Herb Vinegar (page 68)

¼ cup olive oil

⅓ cup wild onions, grated

½ teaspoon coltsfoot ash

1 teaspoon young milkweed shoots, chopped

½ teaspoon wild mustard powder

2 tablespoons honey

1 cup wild mushrooms, cut in bite-size pieces

Place all ingredients except mushrooms in a large saucepan over moderate heat. Bring to a full boil.

Add mushrooms, stirring to coat well. Reduce heat and simmer very gently for 10 minutes.

Remove from heat. Stir. Cover pan with a heavy towel and set in a warm place to cool gradually. Let stand overnight.

Drain cooled mushrooms and discard liquid. Store in a covered jar in the refrigerator. Serve cold.

ELK HEART SPREAD

1   tablespoon olive oil

1   clove garlic, minced

2   wild onions, chopped

½   elk heart, cleaned, trimmed, and diced

1   egg, boiled almost hard

1   tablespoon wild rice flour

1   teaspoon Wild Vegetable Stock (page 77)

½   teaspoon coltsfoot ash

Heat olive oil in a heavy skillet. Add garlic and wild onion. Sauté lightly.

Push sautéed garlic and onion to one side. Add elk heart and sauté until lightly browned on all sides.

Place sautéed garlic, onion, and elk heart in a blender with all remaining ingredients. Blend to a smooth spread, adding more stock if necessary. Chill before serving.

MARINATED JERKY

¼   pound venison jerky

1   wild onion, sliced

½   teaspoon coltsfoot ash

1   teaspoon peppergrass seeds

2   tablespoons Wild Herb Vinegar (page 68)

1   cup yogurt

Break jerky into bite-size pieces. Place in a bowl, alternated with wild onion slices. Sprinkle with coltsfoot ash and peppergrass seeds.

Pour Wild Herb Vinegar over seasoned jerky and wild onion. Let stand, covered, at room temperature about 3 hours.

Place bowl in refrigerator and chill thoroughly. Serve scooped onto lettuce, amaranth, or similar green leaves. Top with yogurt.

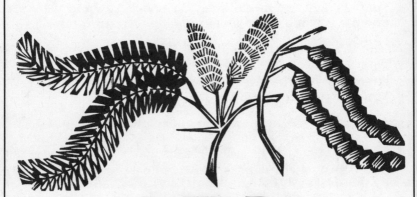

CHAPTER TWO

WILD BEVERAGES

As with appetizers, there is a wide range of wild beverages, from restful and mild to invigorating and spicy. Parp says people often overdo the processes of preparing wild beverages. It's easy to boil the flavor from delicate berries or brew roots down to the bitter dregs. Accordingly, we have experimented with the simplest and most direct methods of producing wild beverages. We have also largely avoided those berries and roots that require excessive processing to be safe or palatable. Again, we caution the reader to be certain of identification by consulting reliable field guides and knowledgeable authorities. With uncooked wild beverages, it is often especially important to be certain that the berry or plant is properly in season. Even in full season, fruit and other plant parts vary considerably in taste. One bush may produce harsh, inedible berries while another may produce the finest berries just a few feet away. This is generally true of all wild foods.

WILD
BEVERAGES

WILD BERRY-MINT SMOOTHY

There are many possibilities for invention and variation using this basic recipe. This is an ideal and healthful alternative to the milk shake or malt.

> 2 cups fresh, whole wild berries
>
> ¼ cup mild honey
>
> ½ teaspoon spicebush
>
> 1 teaspoon lemon juice
>
> ½ teaspoon wild mint, crushed
>
> 1½ cups soy milk (*or* more)
>
> ½ cup ice, cracked

Place all ingredients in a blender and blend until smooth. Serve in chilled glasses.

Yield: *2 servings*

MANZANITA CIDER

> 1 quart water
>
> 1 quart manzanita berries
>
> 2 cups ice-cold water

Bring 1 quart water to a hard boil in a kettle. Add manzanita berries. Boil 10 minutes.

Drain berries and crush thoroughly. Add the cold water and stir. Add more cold water if required. Serve cold.

Yield: *10 servings*

MESQUITE DRINK

- 2 cups water
- 1 cup mesquite pods
- 1 quart cold water

Bring 2 cups water to a hard boil in a kettle. Add mesquite pods. Boil 20 minutes.

Drain mesquite pods. Place in kettle and cover with 1 quart cold water. Mash pods thoroughly in water.

Strain liquid and pour into a chilled pitcher. Refrigerate but do not add ice. Serve cold.

Yield: *6 servings*

PIPSISSEWA (PRINCE'S PINE) PUNCH

- 1 cup pipsissewa leaves and roots, chopped
- ½ cup rose hips
- 2 quarts water
- 2 tablespoons honey

Combine all ingredients in a large kettle. Bring to a boil over high heat. Boil 15 minutes.

Allow to cool, then strain. Add ice and serve cold.

Yield: *10 servings*

JOJOBA COFFEE

The oil of jojoba nuts is widely used as a natural skin treatment and is available in many specialty shops. Although the nuts themselves may be eaten raw or roasted, they are quite bitter. Jojoba oil contains a high percentage of the stimulant tannin, and the nuts may be used to prepare a coffee substitute which some people say is good for dry skin. We have our doubts, but it surely is a stimulating beverage.

½ cup jojoba nuts, roasted

1 egg yolk, hard-boiled

1 tablespoon lemon (*or* orange) juice

1 quart boiling water

steamed milk to taste

warm honey to taste

Use a coffee grinder to grind the nuts as fine as possible. Because of the heavy oil content, the grind will be wet rather than powdery.

In a mixing bowl, combine the ground nuts with the egg yolk and the lemon juice. Mash with a fork to mix well.

Place the mash in the boiling water. Boil hard for 1 minute, then reduce heat and simmer 6 minutes longer. Strain through cheesecloth and serve hot with the milk and honey.

Yield: *4 servings*

A SUBSTITUTE
HOT CHOCOLATE

Purple avens, or chocolate root *(Geum rivale),* is found throughout most of North America but receives very little attention in the literature of wild edibles. This is unfortunate for the roots can make a reasonable substitute for hot chocolate. The plant is easy to identify with the aid of a good field guide and, since only the root is desirable, it can be foraged most of the year.

> 1   cup purple avens, chopped
> 3   cups rapidly boiling water
> ½   cup dark honey
> ⅓   cup skim milk

Place chopped root in a cold kettle. Cover with the water. Boil, stirring occasionally, for 2 hours. Add more boiling water as necessary.

Strain liquid and discard boiled root material. Stir in honey and skim milk. Serve hot.

Yield: *4 servings*

WILD BEVERAGES

CHICKORY OR DANDELION BREW

This is the traditional method of brewing chicory or dandelion as a coffee substitute. We use chicory mixed with coffee, but many people come to prefer chicory brewed by itself. Some use dandelion roots and follow these same instructions for dandelion brew.

> 3 cups fresh chicory (*or* dandelion) root
>
> 1 quart water
>
> 1 tablespoon cold water
>
> mild honey to taste

Preheat oven to 275°F.

Wash chicory root under warm running water. Spread on a baking sheet and place in oven until the roots are dark brown all the way through.

For each pot of brew, use a coffee grinder to grind enough to produce ¼ cup grounds (more or less to taste).

Heat water in a kettle until almost boiling. Reduce heat. Do not allow to boil.

Pour ground roots onto hot water. Keep kettle over very low heat for 10 minutes.

Remove kettle from heat and allow to settle. Add water. Dip brew from kettle without disturbing the grounds. Serve with honey.

BERRY-CURRANT PUNCH

    2 cups fresh berries
    6 cups currants
    ½ gallon cold water
    ¼ cup light honey

Purée combined berries and currants in a blender. Pour unstrained into a large pot.

Add water. Place over very low heat and bring to a simmer. Stir in honey and simmer just long enough to blend well.

Strain liquid and serve chilled.

Yield: *10 servings*

BERRY LEMONADE

    1 cup squaw bush berries
    1 quart cold water
    3 tablespoons light honey

Place berries and 2 cups of the water in a blender. Blend thoroughly. Strain through 3 layers of cheesecloth. Add honey.

Pour drink into a pitcher. Add remaining water and ice. Stir, cover, and refrigerate. Serve cold.

Yield: *6 servings*

**WILD
BEVERAGES**

ROSE HIP TEA

1 tablespoon fresh rose hips (*or* ½ tablespoon dry rose hips)

1 pot very hot water

honey to taste

lemon to taste

Place rose hips in a dry, preheated ceramic teapot.

Cover with the water and steep 5 minutes. Serve with honey, or honey and lemon.

Yield: *4 servings*

SPICEBUSH TEA

1 quart water

½ cup fresh leaves and stems of young spicebush shrub

cinnamon sticks to taste

honey to taste

Bring water to a hard boil. Place spicebush pieces in a dry, preheated teapot.

Pour boiling water over spicebush. Keep hot for 20 minutes. Serve hot with cinnamon sticks and honey.

Yield: *4 servings*

FIREWEED TEA

This is one of the few instances where older wild plants are best. While you're gathering young fireweed for use as greens, take a few select older plants, or return for them later in the season. A small sack of mature fireweed plants will provide many pots of tea. To use, strip the leaves, dry well, and partially crumble.

2 – 3 **tablespoons fireweed leaves, dried**

1 **pot boiling water**

½ **teaspoon honey per cup (optional)**

Place fireweed leaves in a dry, preheated ceramic teapot.

Fill pot with the water. Steep 10 – 12 minutes. Serve with honey.

Yield: *4 servings*

clover

WILD BEVERAGES

STINGING NETTLE TEA

Stinging nettle is especially high in vitamins A and C, making it a fine plant from which to brew a healthful tea. Collect young plants, no more than 10 inches tall. Dry the plants thoroughly, then rub them to loosen the leaves from the stalks. Use 2 teaspoons of the crumbled leaves per pot and follow the procedure for Violet Tea below.

VIOLET TEA

2 teaspoons violet leaves, dried

1 pot very hot water

Place violet leaves in a dry, preheated ceramic teapot. Add the water. Steep 7 – 10 minutes and serve.

Yield: *4 servings*

CONIFER TEA

All the members of the Pine family produce needles that make wonderful tea. True hemlock is most commonly used for this purpose. New leaves are best but any will do, especially if you're cold and lost in the woods.

2 tablespoons hemlock (*or* other conifer) needles

3 cups boiling water

lemon and honey (optional)

Place needles in a warmed kettle or pot. Cover with the water. Steep 7 – 10 minutes.

Strain, if desired, and serve hot with lemon and honey.

Yield: *3 – 4 servings*

HUNTER'S MOON

This drink is said to be just the thing for hunters heading out by moonlight at 2:30 A.M.

¾ cup cider vinegar

⅓ cup molasses

3 tablespoons dark honey

6 cups cold water

1 teaspoon ground ginger (*or* 1 small cube ginger root)

½ teaspoon spicebush

cinnamon sticks or lemon slices (optional)

Purée all ingredients in a blender. Serve hot, with cinnamon sticks, or chilled, with lemon slices.

Yield: *6 servings*

CHAPTER THREE

RAW WILD VEGETABLES, SALADS, AND DRESSINGS

This chapter is devoted to wild plants that can be eaten raw. See Chapter Eleven for wild plants that can be cooked as greens or as vegetables.

In both chapters and throughout this book we emphasize those edible plants that are common in most areas of North America, while avoiding those that may be readily confused with poisonous plants. Of necessity, there are a few exceptions. Common camas, for example, may be confused with death camas if the collector has done no homework at all. But common camas is a fine edible plant and if the collector is aware that common camas always bears bright blue flowers and death camas light green, white, or gray green flowers, there is no danger. This underscores our insistence on the need for a good field guide and competent field identification.

Field identification is complicated by the fact that very often you'll be looking for young shoots and immature plants: many plants are edible in immature forms and inedible as mature plants. Since one young shoot looks much like another, how do you tell them apart?

Proper plant identification demands much attention and effort over a considerable period of time. To be safe with young plants, one should first locate a likely growing area. For example, if you think you've identified young fireweed shoots, pick only a few the first time out. Take them home, dry them in a book, label them, and prepare an information card describing the area where they were found and the appearance of the

plant in detail. Later, when mature plants are available for easier identification, pick, dry, and label them. Match them with the tentatively identified shoots. If you were correct, you can carefully identify the next spring's new shoots by comparing them with the dried and pressed specimens of the previous year.

In general, wild plants are no more dangerous than domestic plants. Many of the vegetables and leafy greens which we commonly consume may have extremely toxic effects if eaten in great quantity, processed improperly, or grown in areas where fertilizers, insecticides, or herbicides are present. This is equally true of most edible wild plants. We urge you never to overindulge in any wild edible. We especially urge you never to collect food plants near an area that has been fertilized.

This caution against fertilizers is most important, no matter how organic the fertilizer is supposed to be. Fertilizers may cause plants to absorb and accumulate toxic levels of nitrates and other poisons. This is sometimes even truer of wild food plants than domestic varieties, and wild plants are less apt to show telltale distress signs when they accumulate high levels of poisons from chemical insecticides, herbicides, or industrial pollution. The only reasonable precaution against nitrate poisoning is to be familiar with your collecting area and avoid fertilized and sprayed areas.

Be alert for a dust or film on wild plants in populous areas; wash them thoroughly. To avoid ingesting lead and other exhaust pollutants, don't collect food plants from busy roadsides. Also, stay away from plants that grow in areas that are or were once waste disposal sites.

SALAD INGREDIENTS

Give greens a simple scrubbing and rinsing in cold water. Roots should be especially well scrubbed, preferably with a stainless steel scouring pad (no detergent, of course) and running water. Some roots obviously should be thoroughly scraped or peeled before eating. Most of the following wild plants may also be cooked and will reappear in Chapter Eleven with details on blanching and other procedures. Again, we urge you to consult authoritative field guides and to avoid areas that may have been treated with any kind of fertilizer, pesticide, insecticide, or herbicide.

Although we present several salad recipes in this chapter, the possibilities for using the ingredients described in the following section are endless. We suggest that you experiment broadly with any combination of these salad ingredients, as long as each single plant is used sparingly. Parp says the key to good salads, and good health, is moderation. Also, you'll find that salads work best if only three or four leafy greens are used, balanced by a flavorful combination of shoots, buds, and seeds.

SALAD GREENS, STEMS, AND SPROUTS

Bracken (fiddleheads, fiddle necks, brake fern).
Pteridium aquilinum

Not recommended. Bracken is well known among foragers as fiddleheads and much has been written about the plant. We find, however, that bracken is not as tasty as its reputation suggests and, considering that recent

information proves it to contain a carcinogen, we rely on other ingredients for our wild salad.

Broad-leaf plantain (Indian wheat, plantain).
Plantago major

For an unusual mushroomlike taste in salads, use only the tender portions of the youngest plantain leaves, discarding the rest. Flavor is improved by blanching a plant for several days. Avoid overdoing the taste of this plant by using only moderate amounts in salads. Dry surplus leaves to use for tea or as a potherb in winter stews and soups.

Cattail. *Typha latifolia*

Cattails produce foods that are available throughout the year in one form or another and have been used and appreciated by Native American groups. For salads, collect young early-summer shoots by cutting them away from the root stocks. Peel off the outer leaves and use the tender, inner portion chopped into small, bean-like pieces.

Chicory. *Cichorium intybus*

Chicory is a well-known edible, especially as a coffee substitute or adulterant. Very young shoots and leaves, blanched for three or four days, are excellent when chopped into salads. For an added bonus, transplant chicory indoors to provide shoots throughout the winter. Blanching precludes most of the bitter taste, but it is best to balance chicory with sweeter leafy greens. This is, however, one plant that may be eaten in quantity (providing the above instructions are noted) without danger or discomfort.

Dandelion. *Taraxacum officinale*

Dandelion enjoys a fair reputation as a salad green but is quite bitter and strong tasting. The flavor can be tamed by gathering only very young plants, or leaves from very young plants growing in shaded areas. The lighter the color the better the taste. Blanching also helps but is not as practical with dandelion as with other plants. In any case, collect leaves and plants before flowers appear. After that, the leaves are far too tough and bitter to be any good at all. To offset the bitter taste, use dandelion only sparingly in salads. Dandelion does well when transplanted indoors to an area with little or no sunlight. The plants thrive all winter and produce pale, almost white leaves that are excellent in winter salads. See the Index for other uses of the plant.

Heron's bill (alfilaria, stork's bill). *Erodium cicutarium*

As one of the first signs of spring, heron's bill is an ingredient for the year's earliest salads. The buds appear even before the warm weather and are a great aid in identification. Young plants with buds or new flowers may be chopped and added to salads.

Horsetails (scouring rush, foxtail). *Equisetum* spp.

Though this common plant is widely known, relatively few realize that it is edible. The outer layer which contains an indigestible and poisonous silicon must be pulled away. Inside, just under the tough outer skin, you'll find a juicy, nutritious pulp that can be eaten raw. Chop the pulp and use it sparingly in salads, rather like a soft bean.

Miner's lettuce (Indian lettuce). *Montia perfoliata*

This beautiful and unusual plant is the best substitute for lettuce in the wild world. Unfortunately, it is primarily a Western plant and we have not heard of it being found in the East. It could probably be cultivated, however, and would be well worth the effort. The stems and leaves are tender, succulent, and very nutritious. Gathered when young in very early spring, it makes a refreshing addition to any wild salad. The leaves toughen considerably through the summer and soon pass the salad stage and must be steamed to be edible. Since miner's lettuce does not keep well, and wilts under refrigeration, it must be used soon after picking.

Mountain sorrel (Alpine sorrel). *Oxyria digyna*

Mountain sorrel is high in vitamin C and is fine for salads at any age. The raw leaves should be torn or shredded into small pieces and combined, in moderation, with sweeter ingredients for a balanced salad. You can dry and store the leaves for winter use in salads or as a potherb. Mountain sorrel is not related to the other sorrels except in its taste, which though rather sour is palatable.

Sheep sorrel (wood-sorrel, sour grass). *Oxalis acetosella*

As its Latin name indicates, this plant contains oxalic acid and can cause mild stomach or intestinal irritation, unless used sparingly. Of course, this is also true of many domestic herbs found in the average kitchen. Fresh young leaves are best, though tender stems may also be chopped and included in salads. The effect is a sour taste which can be quite delicious if balanced with bland or slightly sweet greens. French country cooking relies heavily on sheep sorrel, especially in soups and omelets.

Stonecrop (king's crown, queen's crown). *Sedum* spp.

Various species of stonecrop are widespread in North America, and found, as the common name implies, on rocky ledges, cliffs, and outcrops. Only the youngest shoots and leaves are edible. They are delicious torn or shredded into salads in moderate amounts.

Sweet clover (red clover). *Trifolium pratense*

A few sprigs of fresh, young sweet clover will add protein to a salad and serve as an attractive garnish. New greens are available in abundance through its season. If

you wish to use more than a few sprigs, first soak them in a mixture of one cup Wild Herb Vinegar (see page 68) and one tablespoon lemon juice for two or three hours. This process renders them digestible but does not completely destroy the crispness of the leaves.

Violet (pansy violet, wild pansy). *Viola pedunculate*

All species of violet, wild and domestic, are edible either raw or cooked and are a welcome addition to any wild salad. Check the Index for other uses of this versatile plant. The mild leaves and buds of young spring plants are the best for salads, even when included with stronger tasting ingredients. Although best in spring, violet is one plant that tastes good in all seasons.

Watercress. *Nasturtium officinale*

Euell Gibbons called watercress the "king of wild salad plants" and he was surely correct in that. It has a pungent, zesty flavor that will bring out the best in almost any kind of salad. Pick watercress just above the surface of the water. Recent concern over polluted waters has given watercress a bad name and certainly it should be gathered with caution. We are able to do our gathering in an area of clean creeks, rivers, and pools. Do not pick it from water that you believe to be polluted.

Waterleaf. *Hydrophyllum occidentale*

You'll need a good field guide and some patience to identify this plant, but it's worth the trouble. Use only the young shoots. Cut off at both ends and chop into pieces for salads. It's refreshing and a delicious addition to any crisp, raw salad.

Wild cabbage (squaw cabbage). *Caulanthus crassicaulis*

The leaves of wild cabbage resemble those of the domestic variety but don't grow in as tight a head. Unlike domestic cabbage, wild cabbage must be cooked before eating. Cooked, shredded, and chilled, it may be used much as boiled cabbage and makes a useful salad ingredient. To cook, cover young leaves with boiling water and let stand five minutes. Drain, then rinse in cold water while gently squeezing. Repeat twice.

Wild celery. *Apium graveolens*

The distinction between wild celery and domestic celery is merely a matter of cultivation. Definitely avoid collecting in fertilized areas. Wherever you collect it, be sure to remove and discard the tops of the plants, which likely contain nitrates in dangerous amounts. This is equally true of domestic celery. With this said, young stalks are safe. Wash them well in cold water, chop, and add to salads.

Wild lettuce (chicory lettuce, prickly lettuce). *Lactuca* spp.

Wild lettuce is closely related to our domestic lettuce but is not quite as good unless very young seedling plants are blanched for several days. Miner's lettuce is actually a better salad green, although wild lettuce will appear more appetizing to people unused to wild salads. After blanching by covering with a basket for a few days, use the entire young plant. Cut it with scissors and use as a leafy base just as you would use domestic lettuce, but less generously because of its rather bitter taste.

FLOWERS AND BUDS

Milkweed (showy milkweed). *Asclepias speciosa*

There is a great difference between edible milkweed and the plant known as poison milkweed *(Asclepias subverticillata);* luckily, no one equipped with a field guide should confuse the two. Edible milkweed is a broad-leaved plant; poison milkweed is not. Only the flowers should be eaten raw, and then only in moderation, but they are an attractive addition to wild salads. Young shoots are good in salads if you cook, then cool them first (see cooking instructions in Chapter Eleven).

Fireweed. *Epilobium angustifolium*

Some people enjoy fireweed leaves in salads. Young flower stalks in the bud stage are even better. If you wish to use young shoots in salads, it's best to cook them first in steam, then chop them into small pieces.

Indian paintbrush. *Castilleja californica*

This herb and its relatives produce tasty and beautiful flowers that may be picked from the plants and eaten raw in salads or used as a garnish. Although primarily a southwest regional plant, it does occur in other areas and is so well known in the West that we, as Westerners, couldn't bear to leave it out. The plant can absorb dangerous levels of selenium in western soils so it should be consumed in moderation.

Mallow (cheese-weed). *Malva neglecta*

Mallow is often called cheese-weed, but this nickname has nothing to do with the taste of the plant: the green fruits are shaped somewhat like cheese rounds. Mallow makes good snacks but tastes even better in salads or soups. Raw, they are crisp, refreshing, and somewhat sweet. Use them along with ground cherries or sliced Jerusalem artichokes to complement tossed salads.

Wild rose. *Rosa* spp.

The buds of the wild rose, known as rose hips, are edible as picked and are exceptionally high in vitamin C. Some shrubs produce softer, moister, more palatable buds than others. You might complain of stomach cramps after ingesting a peck of rose hips, so eat them in moderation. To use raw rose hips in salads, slit them lengthways and remove the inner seed portion. Then cut off the blossom end and arrange on top of salad greens as an attractive garnish.

BULBS, TUBERS, AND ROOTS

Bulrush (tule). *Scirpus* spp.

Try to gather roots with a new bud on the end. Raw young rootstocks are good peeled and chopped into tossed salads, but older ones should be cooked first.

Jerusalem artichoke (sunchoke). *Helianthus tuberosus*

No doubt the most famous of all sunflowers, possibly of all wild edibles, Jerusalem artichokes produce large tubers that are excellent when sliced raw into salads. There are several other perennial sunflowers that produce similar tubers, though none so large or tasty as the Jerusalem artichoke. Even people who must avoid starch can eat them; although they do not store well, they may be gathered any time after the first frost and throughout the winter and spring. Identify your foraging area while the plant is in flower, then return in fall and winter to collect (see Index for other entries).

Lily (many common names and varieties). *Lilium* spp.

All lilies produce edible bulbs that may be eaten raw, alone or in salads. Obviously, lilies are beautiful plants and should only be used as food in those areas where they are truly plentiful or cultivated. Lilies do well in cultivation and many people raise them primarily as food. For an unusual, somewhat spicy flavor in salads, slice or chop the bulbs and combine with wild onions, watercress, and miner's lettuce. Beginners should be careful to make a positive identification before eating.

Nut grass (yellow nut grass, chufa). *Cyperus esculentus*

This is a common, widespread, and easily identified plant. The roots bear tubers that you can cut off, peel, and eat raw, either alone or in salads. As the common name implies, the tubers have a nutlike taste that can do much for an otherwise flat-tasting wild salad. No farmer is likely to object if you ask permission to gather them in cultivated areas but be sure you do your collecting on an organic farm that hasn't seen insecticides for several years.

Springbeauty (fairy spuds). *Claytonia* spp.

In areas where it grows in abundance, springbeauty is a popular salad ingredient. In many areas, however, it is scarce and, since it is a very attractive flowering plant, should probably be spared. Sliced raw in salads, springbeauty corms taste crisp and refreshing. Euell Gibbons suggests harvesting only the largest tubers and replanting the smaller ones to encourage more plants. This seems a reasonable approach.

Sweet clover (red clover). *Trifolium pratense*

We include sweet clover in this section on roots because the roots of the plant contain the most nutrition. It also appears in the salad greens section because it would be silly to waste the tops. Raw sweet clover is very high in protein and other nutrients and is delicious in salads. If your system is accustomed to raw wild plants, you can safely eat sizable amounts of clover, flowers included.

Wild caraway (swamproot, yampa).
Perideridia spp.

Although it is a member of the Carrot family, there is little danger of confusing wild caraway with poisonous plants. Wild caraway is one of the finest edible wild plants and a favorite among foragers, both modern and primitive. Use raw roots in salads after washing them under cold running water and peeling. They have a sweet flavor, rather like the best parsnips, and give a delicious nutlike taste to wild salads. The roots will keep very well for use in winter salads.

Wild carrot (Queen Anne's lace, carrot weed).
Daucus carota

Do not eat any part of a wild plant that resembles a carrot unless you are certain you know what you're doing. We refer to this plant frequently because it is common and useful, but it is also the most dangerous for the novice to collect. Other members of the Carrot family include *Cicuta donglasii* and *Conium maculatum* (poison hemlock), both extremely poisonous plants. One bite is usually fatal. There are easy and unmistakable means of distinguishing between the wild carrot and poison hemlock, and you should be very familiar with these distinctions before collecting. As a general rule, the presence of obvious hairs on stems and leaves indicates a safe carrot, but we urge you to read thoroughly on this subject in a good field guide.

Only the youngest, first-year plants are good, sliced raw into salads.

Wild onion. *Allium* and *Brodiaea* spp.

All varieties of both the *Allium* and *Brodiaea* species produce edible bulbs with various degrees of onion flavor. Both genera are classified in the Amaryllis family and many species are known locally or otherwise as wild onions. Species of *Allium* are probably best, or most acceptable, to the cook who desires an onion taste and consistency. The bulbs should all be treated exactly as we treat domestic onions. Some are more like leeks than onions, while others taste more like garlic. The usual rule is that if it looks, tastes, and smells like an onion, it is an onion, but we still urge the beginning collector to use a competent field guide to be certain of identification. Various U.S. Government Printing Office publications make the risky statement that wild onions are never poisonous. The truth of that statement hinges on the quantity considered: all onions, including domestic onions, are poisonous if eaten in very large quantity. However, it's safe to eat normal amounts. Besides, where would we be without them? Moderation, says Parp, in onions as in all things. Wild onions may be chopped, sliced, or dried for use in salads. One small onion, eaten plain and raw, seems to increase energy and alertness.

Refer to Chapter Eleven for additional information on gathering, cooking, and eating wild onions.

COOKED SPRING SALAD

1   bunch young amaranth leaves, steamed

½   cup heron's bill, steamed

½   cup wild asparagus, steamed

¼   cup springbeauty tubers, lightly boiled

Rinse all ingredients in cold water and drain well.

Place in a salad bowl and toss together. Serve with oil and vinegar dressing.

SPRING SALAD

1   cup miner's lettuce, shredded

⅓   cup mountain sorrel

⅓   cup watercress

⅓   cup nut grass tubers

Combine all ingredients in a salad bowl. Toss together. Serve very lightly dressed.

SUMMER SALAD

- ½ cup wild lettuce
- ½ cup ground cherries
- ¼ cup violet leaves and buds
- ¼ cup mixed watercress and mountain sorrel

Rinse all ingredients under cold running water and drain well.

Place in a salad bowl and toss together. Serve with oil and vinegar or Wild French Dressing (page 69).

AUTUMN SALAD

- 1 cup Jerusalem artichoke, boiled, cooled, and diced
- ½ cup wild onions, diced
- ¼ cup wild carrots (*or* wild caraway), grated
- ½ cup wild apple, cut in pieces
- ¼ cup wild cabbage, grated
- 2 stalks wild celery, chopped

Place all ingredients in a salad bowl and toss together. Serve with olive oil and Wild Herb Vinegar (page 68).

WINTER SALAD

- 1 cup chestnuts, boiled and sliced
- ¼ cup roasted piñon (*or* pine) nuts
- ¼ cup preserved sweet tubers
- 2 tablespoons rose hips, dried
- ⅓ cup wild cabbage, grated
- 1 tablespoon amaranth seeds
- 3 tablespoons olive oil
- 1 teaspoon dill

Place all ingredients in a salad bowl and toss together.
Serve immediately.

jerusalem artichoke

PLANTAIN SALAD

- ¾ cup young plantain leaves, blanched
- ⅓ cup cattail shoots, chopped
- 1 lily bulb, sliced
- 1 young wild carrot, chopped
- 1 tablespoon peppergrass seeds

Combine all ingredients in a salad bowl and toss together. Serve with Wild French Dressing (page 69).

VIOLET SALAD

- 1 bunch miner's lettuce (*or* wild lettuce *or* amaranth leaves)
- ½ cup ground cherries, sliced in half
- ⅓ cup wild carrots, chopped
- ¼ cup violet leaves, shredded
- 2 tablespoons violet buds
- 1 tablespoon lemon juice

Toss all plant ingredients together. Add lemon juice and dressing.

WILD CABBAGE SLAW

    3   cups wild cabbage, shredded and cooked

3 or 4 wild onions, chopped fine

    ½   cup sprouts

    ½   sunchoke, grated

    1   tablespoon watercress, diced

Toss all ingredients together and serve with any dressing.

CHICKWEED SALAD

Since young chickweed plants can usually be found in 3 seasons of the year, this is a salad you'll be able to enjoy often.

    ½   pound young chickweed stems

    1   clove garlic, minced

2 or 3 wild onions, chopped

    4   tablespoons safflower oil

    3   tablespoons lemon juice

4 or 5 ground cherries, sliced

    2   hard-boiled eggs, sliced

Trim, wash, and drain chickweed stems. Cut into small pieces.

Combine garlic, onions, oil, and lemon juice. Pour over chickweed stems. Toss and garnish with ground cherries and eggs.

YOGURT SALAD

- 1 **cup soybeans, cooked**
- 1 **cup wild greens, steamed (*or* tubers *or* roots, boiled)**
- ¼ **cup lilac buds (*or* rose hips)**
- ½ **cup cheese, grated**
- ½ **teaspoon spicebush**
- ¼ **teaspoon coltsfoot ash**
- 1 **cup yogurt**
- 1 **tablespoon peppergrass seeds**

Toss together all ingredients except yogurt and seeds. Add yogurt by spoonfuls. Sprinkle with seeds.

WILD FRUIT SALAD

Use fresh or frozen fruit.

¼ cup wild berries, as available

½ cup wild apples, diced

1 cup coconut, shredded

1 tablespoon lemon juice

¼ cup light honey

1 cup yogurt

1 head lettuce

2 tablespoons wild mint, chopped

Place berries, apples, and coconut in a large bowl and toss together. Add lemon juice, honey, and yogurt. Cover and refrigerate 3 hours.

Arrange lettuce on a large, chilled salad platter. Place fruit mixture in center. Sprinkle with wild mint. Serve immediately.

MOLDED WILD CARROT SALAD

1 lemon

1 tablespoon unflavored gelatin

1½ cups apple cider, heated

1½ cups wild carrots, grated

½ cup currants

¼ cup amaranth seeds

Peel lemon and squeeze pulp. Reserve pulp and juice together. Grate half of the peel.

Place gelatin in lemon juice mixture to soften. Place cider in a bowl.

Add lemon juice mixture and gelatin to cider and stir to dissolve gelatin. Allow to cool 20 minutes.

Stir wild carrots, grated peel, and currants into gelatin mixture. Pour into mold and chill. Sprinkle with amaranth seeds just before serving.

DANDELION SALAD

- 1 bunch very young, light-colored (*or* blanched) dandelion leaves
- 1 wild onion, sliced very thin
- ⅓ cup dandelion root, chopped
- 2 tablespoons sweet cicely root, chopped
- 2 tablespoons lemon (*or* orange) juice

Toss plant ingredients together. Sprinkle with lemon juice. Serve immediately.

WILD HERB VINEGAR

You can make your own herb vinegar with wild herbs and ordinary cider vinegar. This concoction is a delicious ingredient in dressings for wild greens.

- 1 gallon cider vinegar
- ¼ cup peppergrass seeds
- ½ cup wild onions, chopped
- ¼ cup wild chives, chopped
- 1 teaspoon wild dill
- 1 small bunch wild rosemary leaves and top stems
- 1 small bunch wild thyme leaves and top stems
- 1 salsify root, scraped
- ¼ cup wild parsley leaves, dried

Combine all ingredients in a large earthenware bowl. Allow to set at room temperature 3 hours.

Stir well and pour into widemouthed jars. Seal and store 30 days in a cool, dark place.

Strain liquid through cheesecloth and seal in hot sterile jars. Discard solids. Use as herb vinegar in any recipe or combine with salad oil for oil and vinegar dressing.

WILD FRENCH DRESSING

1 teaspoon peppergrass seeds

¼ teaspoon coltsfoot ash

3 tablespoons olive oil

3 tablespoons Wild Herb Vinegar (page 68)

¼ teaspoon wild mustard powder

3 tablespoons safflower oil

1 clove garlic, peeled

In a small bowl, combine peppergrass seeds, coltsfoot ash, 1 tablespoon olive oil, 1 tablespoon Wild Herb Vinegar, and the wild mustard powder. Beat with a whisk until smooth.

Add another tablespoon olive oil and 1 tablespoon safflower oil. Blend well with whisk.

Add remaining oil and vinegar. Beat with whisk again. Pour dressing into a jar, drop in garlic, and cover with screw lid. Store in refrigerator overnight. Shake before serving.

CHAPTER FOUR

STOCKS
AND
SOUPS

Nothing so distinguishes a good and serious cook as do fine stocks and soups and this is perhaps especially true of those who cook wild meats and vegetables. In the modern, sterile grocery, many of the ingredients essential to good stocks and soups are banned from display. Few stores offer such wonders as jaw bones, soft vegetables, and turkey heads. Yet these are the kinds of goods fine cooks cherish "for the pot."

Always prepare stocks long before you plan to use them. Of the various wild stocks, fowl and game stocks may be substituted for chicken, duck, or beef stocks in any recipe. Bear stock replaces veal or ham stock and may be used in bean soups without the danger of chemicals found in grocery hams. Small-game stocks are most interesting, and experiments in the preparation and use of these stocks are fascinating and rewarding. Such experiments, in ancient Europe, became the basis for fine French cuisine.

BASIC DARK GAME STOCK

It's fascinating to experiment with the ingredients that go into wild stock. The basic procedure is to start with cold water in a pot, add the ingredients, bring to a boil, then reduce the heat and simmer very slowly, uncovered. It's best to prepare stock well in advance, allowing yourself time to chill it and skim the fat before you need to use it. (Remember to reserve the drippings from wildfowl stocks.) Stocks may be frozen in pans, then removed from the pans, wrapped in labeled packages, and returned to the freezer. Good cooks who put time into their meals always keep a variety of frozen stocks on hand. Fowl or game stocks may be substituted for chicken, duck, or beef stocks in any recipe.

MUSKRAT

4 quarts cold water

5 – 8 pounds small-game bones (*or* venison marrow bones)

1 bay leaf

3 wild carrots, cut in chunks

3 stalks wild celery, cut in chunks

2 sprigs watercress

1 cup ground cherries

1 wild parsnip (*or* wild caraway root), cut in chunks

Place water in a large soup pot. Add all other ingredients.

Place over moderate heat and bring to a boil. Reduce heat and simmer 3 hours, uncovered.

Strain stock. Remove marrow from large bones and stir back into hot stock. Discard all other strained-out ingredients.

Allow stock to cool, uncovered, to room temperature. Then refrigerate 24 hours. Skim fat from chilled stock and reserve. Use stock in soups or freeze for future use.

WILDFOWL STOCK

The successful bird hunter is in a position often envied
by the best and most knowledgeable cooks. There is no
doubt that the parts of game birds often discarded by
hunters—wings, legs, backs, necks, and even heads—
can produce the finest and most useful stock. Such a
stock is an essential ingredient in the finest Continental cuisine. In fact, the less useful an item otherwise,
the more likely it is to produce good stock. The toughest
legs of fowl, for example, are ideal for stock. And old
birds' wings that are beyond hope for table fare are
exactly what you need for good stock. The same is true,
incidentally, of vegetables, either wild or domestic. The
older and less appetizing the vegetable, the better it is
for the stock pot. A good cook is constantly alert for
likely ingredients for the stock pot and wastes far less
food than the cook who does not bother to make stock.
Parp says it's a crime to throw away those tough old
birds' wings or the carcass left after a feast of fowl.

Here is a basic recipe for a clear game stock.

> 3 quarts cold water
>
> 5 pounds game bird carcass, wings, legs,
>   necks, and other spare parts
>
> 2 – 3 stalks wild celery, cut in chunks
>
> ½ cup wild onions, chopped
>
> ½ cup wild carrots, chopped
>
> 1 small bunch watercress

Place cold water in a soup pot.

Place game bird pieces in cold water. Soak for 1 hour.

Add other ingredients. Do not stir. Soak for an hour.

Place pot, uncovered, at the back of a cookstove far from the fire. On a conventional stove, place the pot on an asbestos pad over very low heat.

Allow the pot and its contents to warm very slowly. You need to draw as much as possible out of the ingredients and into the stock. Skim off scum as it rises.

When the pot is uniformly warm, move it closer to the fire (or increase the heat) and very slowly and carefully bring the liquid to a simmer. Do not boil. Do not rush. Skim off all scum immediately, as it rises within the first 30 minutes of simmering. After 30 minutes and after skimming, use a clean piece of cheesecloth to wipe the pot at the level of the liquid.

Simmer very gently, uncovered, for at least 3 hours.

Taking great care not to disturb the ingredients, carefully ladle the liquid through clean, moistened cheesecloth into a large, screw-lid jar. Do not pour the stock.

Leave the strained stock uncovered until cool.

Cover cooled stock tightly and store in the refrigerator. Do not remove grease at this time.

Skim grease from stock. Reheat for use, or freeze.

Yield: *8 cups*

BEAR PAW STOCK

For those hunters who've always wondered what to do with the paws after the claws are removed, Parp offers this recipe for a simple and versatile stock. Similar to veal stock, it can take the place of light stock in any recipe, or substitute for ham stock in bean soup.

4 bear paws, with nails, hair, and skin removed

1 quart rapidly boiling water

4 quarts cold water

6 white peppercorns

1 bay leaf

2 stalks wild celery, chopped

2 wild carrots, chopped

2 wild onions, chopped

2 – 3 sprigs watercress

Place bear paws in a pot. Cover with the boiling water. Rest 3 – 4 minutes, then drain. Discard liquid.

Place the cold water in a large soup pot. Add drained and blanched bear paws and all other ingredients.

Bring almost to a boil over moderate heat. Reduce heat and simmer, uncovered, 3 hours. Strain and cool to room temperature, uncovered. Refrigerate and skim surface after 24 hours.

Yield: *8 cups*

PURE WILD VEGETABLE STOCK

A basic wild vegetable stock has many uses. It is especially good with wild vegetable main dishes, which would be ruined by the use of a game or meat-based stock. Vegetable stock is very simple to make and may be frozen or canned for future use.

    1 cup wild onions, finely chopped

    2 tablespoons oil

    1 teaspoon tarragon

    ½ teaspoon coltsfoot ash (*or* lemon juice)

    ½ cup wild carrots, diced

    ½ cup wild parsnip (*or* wild caraway root), diced

    ¼ cup wild celery stalks, diced

    ¼ cup wild mushrooms, cut in pieces

    1 quart (*or* more) cold water, to cover

Combine all ingredients in a large soup pot.

Bring almost to a boil over moderate heat. Place cover slightly ajar. Lower heat and simmer 2 hours. Strain and chill before freezing or pour into hot, sterile jars and seal.

Yield: *6 cups*

QUICK GAME STOCK

This stock can be prepared in a pressure cooker and be ready for immediate use. Although not as delicious as a traditional stock, it will do when time is short.

   3 tablespoons corn oil

   2 pounds venison, cubed

   1 quart boiling water

   1 venison soup bone

   1 bay leaf

   2 wild carrots, chopped

   2 wild onions, chopped

   2 stalks wild celery, chopped

   2 sprigs watercress

   1 teaspoon peppergrass seeds

  ½ teaspoon coltsfoot ash

Heat oil in a pressure cooker. Add venison and brown.

Add remaining ingredients. Cook at 15 pounds pressure for 45 minutes. Strain and allow stock to cool to room temperature, uncovered. Chill in refrigerator 3 − 4 hours. Skim surface before using.

Yield: *6 cups*

FISH STOCK

The wild and exotic edibles in this recipe make for an unusual fish stock.

  3 tablespoons safflower oil

  ½ cup wild onions, chopped

  ½ cup wild celery stalks, chopped

  ½ cup wild carrots, chopped

  1 teaspoon peppergrass seeds

  ⅓ cup liverberries

  ⅓ cup young milkweed shoots, chopped

  3 tablespoons Wild Herb Vinegar (page 68)

  4 cups cold water

  2 pounds whitefish heads, tails, and trimmings

Heat oil in a large soup pot. Add onions, celery, and carrots. Brown lightly, then reduce heat and cook gently about 5 minutes.

Add remaining ingredients. Increase to moderate heat and simmer uncovered, about 30 minutes. Skim surface as necessary.

Strain and cool to room temperature. Chill thoroughly. Skim surface after chilling. Store in freezer.

Yield: *4 − 6 cups*

ARROWHEAD SOUP

½ pound arrowhead tubers

¼ pound Indian potatoes

3 cups boiling water

1 bunch watercress, chopped

1 cup coconut milk

1 teaspoon safflower oil

¼ teaspoon coltsfoot ash

Place arrowhead tubers and Indian potatoes in boiling water. Boil 15 minutes. Drain, reserving water. Remove scales and peels from tubers and potatoes.

Rub tubers and potatoes together through a fine sieve. Return to cooking water. Add watercress and simmer 10 minutes.

Lower heat and stir in coconut milk, safflower oil, and coltsfoot ash. Continue to heat very gently 3 − 4 minutes. Stir to blend well and serve hot, immediately.

Yield: *4 servings*

WILD ONION SOUP

- 2 tablespoons safflower oil
- 2 cups wild onions, sliced
- 6 cups Wildfowl Stock (page 74) (*or* Wild Vegetable Stock [page 77])
- ½ teaspoon peppergrass seeds
- 2 cups very dry rye bread, in large pieces
- 1 cup Parmesan cheese, grated

Preheat oven to 300°F.

Heat oil in a large casserole dish. Brown wild onion slices.

Add stock and peppergrass seeds. Cover casserole and place in oven for 20 minutes.

Remove cover from casserole dish. Float rye bread pieces on surface of soup and sprinkle generously with grated Parmesan cheese.

Place casserole, uncovered, in oven and bake 15 minutes. Serve hot.

Yield: *4 servings*

WATERCRESS SOUP

6 cups Wildfowl Stock (page 74)

2 cups wild watercress, chopped

1 teaspoon coltsfoot ash

1 tablespoon young milkweed shoots, chopped

Gently heat Wildfowl Stock in a soup pot.

Add other ingredients. Simmer 5 minutes, without boiling. Serve immediately.

Yield: *6 servings*

MUSHROOM SOUP

½ pound wild mushrooms, cut in small pieces

3 cups Wild Vegetable Stock (page 77)

3 tablespoons wild rice flour

½ cup cold water

¼ pound cheddar cheese, grated

Combine mushrooms and cold Wild Vegetable Stock in a soup pot over moderate heat. Bring to the point of boiling, then reduce heat and simmer 30 minutes.

Combine wild rice flour and water, blending well. Stir into hot soup. Simmer 15 minutes.

Pour soup into individual serving bowls. Top with grated cheese. Serve immediately.

Yield: *4 servings*

CURRIED DUCK SOUP

    2   tablespoons safflower oil

    1   teaspoon curry powder

    1   tablespoon flour

    2   cups Wildfowl Stock (page 74)

    ¼   teaspoon paprika

    ½   cup yogurt

    ½   cup cooked duck meat, diced

    1   tablespoon Parp's Wild Chutney (page 103)

    1   tablespoon wild chives, chopped

Heat oil in a soup pot. Use a whisk to thoroughly blend in curry powder and flour.

Add Wildfowl Stock gradually, stirring constantly. Bring to a boil and add paprika. Reduce heat.

When boiling has stopped completely, whisk in yogurt. Cook and stir over low heat 5 – 7 minutes. Do not allow to boil.

Add duck meat and Parp's Wild Chutney and continue to cook another 5 minutes without boiling.

Ladle into serving bowls and garnish with chopped wild chives. Serve immediately.

Yield: *4 servings*

GROUSE SOUP

Most of the meat on a grouse is so tough and full of tendons that it simply isn't good to eat. The wings and backs do make an excellent soup, however, if you haven't already used them for stock. After you've enjoyed the breast meat broiled or roasted, try this.

- 2 grouse, cleaned, breasts removed
- 1 quart cold water
- 1 cup Wildfowl Stock (page 74) (*or* Wild Vegetable Stock [page 77])
- 3 wild onions, chopped
- 2 wild caraway roots, chopped
- 2 wild carrots, chopped
- 2 stalks wild celery, chopped
- 1 teaspoon coltsfoot ash
- 1 teaspoon peppergrass seeds

Cut wings, necks, and backs into large piece. Place in pot and cover with water. Add stock and bring almost to a boil. Reduce heat and simmer 1 hour.

Remove grouse from liquid. Strip off meat and return this to the pot. Add remaining ingredients except coltsfoot ash and peppergrass seeds.

Simmer 1 hour longer. Add seasonings and simmer 15 more minutes. Serve hot.

Yield: *6 servings*

SMALL-GAME SOUP

This recipe will adapt to most dark-meat small game, including squirrel, marmot, and groundhog. For very small animals, decrease the ingredients proportionately.

1−2 small-game animals, cleaned, skinned, and hung

cold water to cover

2 cups Dark Game Stock (page 72) (*or* Wild Vegetable Stock [page 77])

2 wild onions, chopped

2 wild caraway roots, diced

1 bunch wild mustard leaves

6 wild carrots, chopped

1 small bunch watercress

¼ cup violet leaves and buds

1 teaspoon coltsfoot ash

Cut animal into large pieces and place in a soup pot. Add water and stock. Bring to the point of boiling, then reduce heat and simmer 1 hour.

Remove game pieces from liquid. Bone and cut meat into small pieces. Return cubed meat to pot.

Add remaining ingredients. Simmer 1 hour longer, stirring frequently. Serve hot.

Yield: *4 servings*

VENISON-BARLEY SOUP

 4 tablespoons corn oil

 ½ pound venison, cubed

 6 cups Dark Game Stock, chilled (page 72)

 1 tablespoon peppergrass seeds

 1 tablespoon spicebush

 ½ cup wild celery stalks, chopped

 ¼ cup wild onions, chopped

 ¼ cup wild carrots, chopped

 ¼ cup whole barley

 1 cup ground cherries, lightly mashed

 2 tablespoons violet buds, chopped

 1 cup wild mushrooms, sliced

Heat 2 tablespoons oil in a large soup pot. Add venison and sauté until lightly browned on all sides.

Add Dark Game Stock and bring to a boil. Add peppergrass seeds and spicebush. Reduce heat and simmer, covered, for 15 minutes.

Meanwhile, heat remaining oil in a skillet. Add wild celery, onions, and carrots. Sauté lightly, then add to soup.

Stir in barley and simmer, covered, about 1 hour. Add cherries, violet buds, and wild mushrooms. Simmer, uncovered, another 15 minutes, stirring occasionally. Serve hot.

Yield: *6 servings*

WILD CELERY SOUP

    2 tablespoons safflower oil

    2 cups wild celery stalks, chopped

    ½ cup bulrush shoots, chopped

    ½ cup wild onions, chopped

  3½ cups Wildfowl Stock, chilled (page 74) (*or* Wild
       Vegetable Stock [page 77])

    ¾ cup skim milk powder

    ¾ cup water

    ½ cup yogurt

    ½ teaspoon kelp powder

    ½ teaspoon coltsfoot ash

Heat safflower oil in a heavy skillet and sauté wild celery
and bulrush shoots. Remove and reserve ¾ cup of the
combined, sautéed vegetables.

Add chopped wild onions to the skillet and sauté lightly.
Place combined sautéed vegetables in a blender and
purée.

Place puréed vegetables in a soup pot over low heat. Add
Wildfowl Stock.

Combine milk powder and water. Stir into soup. Add
yogurt and reserved, sautéed vegetables. Stir to combine well. Add kelp powder and coltsfoot ash. Heat
thoroughly over low heat, 10 minutes or so, without
boiling. Serve hot.

Yield: *4 servings*

ground cherry

GROUND CHERRY AND GREENBRIER SOUP

    3 tablespoons olive oil
    ½ cup wild onions, chopped
    ¾ cup greenbrier root, diced
    1 clove garlic, minced
    2 tablespoons pith of fireweed stems
    1 teaspoon wild thyme
    1 tablespoon young milkweed shoots, chopped
    2 cups ground cherries, lightly mashed
    3 cups Wild Vegetable Stock (page 77)
    ½ teaspoon coltsfoot ash
    1 tablespoon light honey
    2 tablespoons violet (*or* purslane) flowers and
       buds, chopped

Heat olive oil in a large, heavy skillet. Lightly sauté chopped onions, greenbrier root, and garlic together.

Place sautéed vegetables in a large soup pot. Add fireweed pith, wild thyme, milkweed shoots, ground cherries, and Wild Vegetable Stock. Place over medium heat and bring to a boil. Immediately reduce heat and simmer for 45 minutes.

Stir in coltsfoot ash, honey, and chopped flowers and buds. Simmer another 10 minutes, uncovered. Serve hot.

Yield: *4 servings*

INDIAN POTATO SOUP

This is a basic recipe and any kind of wild tuber or root may be used in various combinations. The other ingredients are flexible as well and may be altered to apply to the particular root or tuber or combination that is the main ingredient. This recipe is suited to Indian potato, sunchoke, parsnip, and similar roots.

    4 cups Indian potatoes, diced

    1 cup wild parsnip (*or* wild caraway root), diced

    ½ cup wild celery stalks, chopped

    ¼ cup wild onions, chopped

    ⅓ cup young milkweed shoots

    1½ quarts cold Wild Vegetable Stock (page 77)

    1 tablespoon peppergrass seeds (*or* watercress)

    1 teaspoon coltsfoot ash

    1 cup skim milk powder

    1 cup cold water

    ½ cup yogurt

Place potatoes, parsnip, celery, onions, milkweed shoots, and Wild Vegetable Stock in a large pot. Place over medium heat and bring to a boil. Immediately reduce heat and simmer for an hour, stirring occasionally.

Stir in peppergrass seeds and coltsfoot ash. Continue simmering.

Combine skim milk and water. Stir into soup. Stir in yogurt. Simmer 5 minutes, without boiling. Serve hot.

Yield: *6 servings*

CREAM OF AMARANTH SOUP

3 cups fresh young amaranth leaves

¾ cup boiling water

1 cup skim milk powder

3 tablespoons wild rice flour

3 cups cold water

2 cups Wild Vegetable Stock (page 77)

½ cup yogurt

2 tablespoons wild onions, grated

1 teaspoon watercress

¼ teaspoon coltsfoot ash

Place amaranth leaves on rack over the boiling water. Steam 5 – 8 minutes. Remove and chop or tear into very small pieces.

In a saucepan, combine skim milk powder and flour with the cold water. Place over low heat. Stir in Wild Vegetable Stock. Continue to heat and stir until mixture thickens, about 10 minutes. Blend in yogurt.

Add amaranth leaves to cream sauce. Stir and cook gently for about 10 minutes, then stir in wild onions, watercress, and coltsfoot ash. Cook another 3 minutes, then serve immediately.

Yield: *6 servings*

BUFFALO IN SAFFRON BROTH

Meatballs

- 1 pound ground buffalo
- ¼ cup acorn (*or* corn) meal
- 1 egg, beaten
- ½ teaspoon coltsfoot ash
- 1 teaspoon peppergrass seeds
- ¼ teaspoon wild mustard powder
- 2 wild onions, chopped
- 1 small stalk wild celery, chopped
- 1 tablespoon corn oil

Saffron broth

- 3 tablespoons corn oil
- ¼ cup wild rice flour
- 2 cups Dark Game Stock, warmed (page 72)
- 7 cups water
- 1 teaspoon saffron
- 2 tablespoons Dark Game Stock, warmed
- 2 tablespoons mint, dried
- 1 teaspoon coltsfoot ash
- 1 teaspoon peppercorns

Have all ingredients at room temperature. In a large mixing bowl, combine all ingredients for buffalo meatballs. Blend well, then shape into meatballs. Brown lightly in hot oil.

Heat corn oil for saffron broth in a large kettle. Mix in flour with a wire whisk. Cook 2−3 minutes, whisking constantly over moderate heat.

Pour in 2 cups Dark Game Stock, whisking energetically. Add water and continue cooking 5 minutes, stirring frequently.

Combine saffron and 2 tablespoons Dark Game Stock. Add this and all remaining ingredients to the kettle. Cook, stirring occasionally, and bring to a boil. Boil 2−3 minutes, then reduce heat to a simmer.

Add browned buffalo meatballs. Simmer 25−30 minutes. Serve hot with rye rolls and tossed salad.

Yield: *4−6 servings*

STOCKS
AND
SOUPS

GAME LIVER SOUP

    3 tablespoons olive oil

    2 wild onions, sliced

    2 cups wild mushrooms, sliced

    ½ pound game liver (venison, porcupine, *or*
       combined small game), cubed

    3 cups Dark Game Stock, chilled (page 72)

    2 eggs, beaten

    2 tablespoons violet (*or* daylily) flowers and buds,
       chopped

    1 teaspoon peppergrass seeds (*or* watercress)

Heat olive oil in a large soup pot. Add sliced onions and
mushrooms. Sauté lightly.

Add cubed liver. Sauté until lightly browned on all
sides. Add Dark Game Stock and bring to a simmer. Do
not boil. Cover tightly and simmer 20 minutes.

Blend in eggs. Add flowers and buds and peppergrass
seeds. Simmer another 10 minutes, stirring occasionally. Serve hot.

Yield: *4 servings*

BEAR-FLAVORED BEAN SOUP

1½ cups dried beans, soaked overnight and drained

6 cups Bear Paw Stock, chilled (page 76)

2 tablespoons corn oil

1 clove garlic, minced

¼ cup wild onions, chopped

½ cup wild celery stalks, chopped

½ cup wild carrots (or greenbrier root), chopped

1 teaspoon peppergrass seeds

¼ teaspoon coltsfoot ash

1 tablespoon daylily flowers and buds, chopped

Place beans in a large soup pot. Add Bear Paw Stock. Place over medium heat and bring to a boil. Reduce heat and simmer, covered.

Meanwhile, heat corn oil in a skillet. Add garlic and wild onions. Sauté lightly, then add wild celery and carrots. Sauté 4–5 minutes, then add to soup. Stir soup and simmer, covered, for 1 hour.

Add peppergrass seeds and coltsfoot ash. Cover and continue to simmer another 30 minutes.

Add daylily flowers and buds. Simmer, uncovered, 15 minutes longer. Serve hot.

Yield: *4–6 servings*

BEAVER TAIL SOUP

To remove the skin from a beaver tail, place tail in a
375°F oven for about 20 – 30 minutes or place the tail
on a grill over an open fire. When the skin scorches and
puffs, it will peel off easily. Then remove the meat from
the bones.

- 3 tablespoons corn oil
- ½ cup wild onions, chopped
- ¼ cup wild celery stalks, chopped
- ¼ cup wild carrots, diced
- ½ cup pith of young fireweed stems
- 1 beaver tail, skinned, boned, and cubed
- 6 cups Bear Paw Stock (page 76) (*or* Wild Vegetable Stock [page 77])
- 2 cups water
- 1 bay leaf
- ⅛ teaspoon wild thyme
- 1 teaspoon spicebush
- 1 teaspoon peppergrass seeds
- ½ cup wild rice, steamed

wild mint to garnish (optional)

Heat corn oil in a large soup kettle. Add wild onions, celery, carrots, and pith of fireweed stems. Sauté lightly.

Add beaver tail meat, Bear Paw Stock, water, and bay leaf. Bring to a boil over moderate heat. Immediately reduce heat and simmer, uncovered, 40 minutes. Skim occasionally.

Add all remaining ingredients. Simmer another 30 minutes. Serve hot, garnished with wild mint.

Yield: *4 – 6 servings*

spice bush

PARP'S WILD SOUP

Here's another of those Parp recipes that begs for imaginative substitutions. This soup will accept leftovers from the refrigerator as well as wild greens, blossoms, roots, or stems.

¼ cup olive oil

½ cup wild onions, chopped

½ cup wild carrots (*or* parsnip), chopped

¼ cup wild celery, chopped

2 tablespoons acorn meal

2 teaspoons curry powder

5 cups Wildfowl Stock (page 74) (*or* Wild Vegetable Stock [page 77])

¼ cup wild apples, diced

⅓ cup liverberries

½ cup wild rice, steamed

¾ cup cooked meat of wildfowl, cubed

½ teaspoon coltsfoot ash

½ teaspoon peppergrass seeds

¼ teaspoon wild thyme

½ cup yogurt

Heat oil in a large soup pot. Add wild onions, carrots, and celery. Sauté very lightly.

Stir in acorn meal and curry powder. Cook about 3 minutes, then add Wildfowl Stock. Simmer over moderate heat for about 45 minutes.

Add all remaining ingredients except yogurt. Simmer 25 – 30 minutes.

Blend in yogurt and simmer very gently for another 2 – 3 minutes. Serve immediately.

Yield: *6 servings*

CHAPTER FIVE

SAUCES, GRAVIES, AND STUFFINGS

Old Parp is pedestrian: his favorite sauce is a gravy—usually simple pan gravy, especially with small game, large game, and fried fowl. He gets a little fancier when it comes to fish, roast fowl, and vegetable dishes.

But whatever your preference, a good sauce or gravy lifts any meal, especially a wild meal, from dry and ordinary to moist and flavorful. Yogurt as a sauce ingredient is largely overlooked and underrated. With few exceptions, it will replace sour cream with healthful and flavorful results. Parp's Ground Cherry Sauce and Wild Chutney are superb original sauces to be used sparingly with all manner of meat and egg dishes.

Many people overspice and overwet stuffings for fish and fowl. The flesh of fish and fowl is delicate and moist and should not be overcome. If you are fortunate enough to have a supply of wild rice, you'll find that Wild Rice Stuffing is incomparable with fish and fowl, while Wild Apple Dressing is superb with all game cuts.

PARP'S GROUND CHERRY SAUCE

- 1 cup fresh, ripe ground cherries, husked
- 3 wild onions, chopped
- ½ teaspoon coriander seeds
- ½ teaspoon chili powder
- ½ teaspoon lemon juice
- ¼ teaspoon basil

Place ground cherries in a saucepan. Add water to cover and bring to the boiling point. Reduce heat and simmer 30 minutes.

Place ground cherries, cooking liquid, and all remaining ingredients in a blender. Blend lightly and season to taste. Serve over meats or as a condiment for wild game sandwiches.

GOOSEBERRY GAME SAUCE

- ½ cup apple cider vinegar
- 2 quarts gooseberries
- 1½ cups dark honey
- 1 teaspoon lemon juice
- 1 teaspoon spicebush
- 1 teaspoon cloves
- ½ teaspoon cinnamon
- ¼ teaspoon cayenne pepper

Place ½ of the vinegar in a kettle. Add 2 cups gooseberries and mash lightly. Place over medium heat.

As mixture heats, add remaining gooseberries and vinegar. Bring to a full boil, then slowly stir in honey.

Add remaining ingredients and return to a full boil. Reduce heat and simmer 1 hour. Pour into prepared jars and seal. Serve with all game dishes.

PARP'S WILD CHUTNEY

This Parp original is tasty with all meats and poultry. It's best, though, with scrambled eggs and leftover game, or with any strong-tasting small game, such as musquash or porcupine. It can be used sparingly, to accent the taste of game, or heavily, to cover it. Use our recommended canning methods to preserve.

- 1 cup fresh gooseberries
- 1 clove garlic, chopped
- 4 cups ground cherries
- 1 cup currants
- ½ cup fresh ginger root
- 1 teaspoon lemon juice
- ¾ cup apple cider vinegar
- 1 cup honey

Heat all ingredients except honey and bring to a gentle boil, stirring occasionally.

Add honey. Lower heat and simmer 45 minutes. Seal chutney in hot, sterilized jars to preserve.

SAUCES,
GRAVIES, AND
STUFFINGS

WILD GAME BROWN SAUCE

  2 tablespoons corn oil

  4 tablespoons wild rice flour

  1 cup Dark Game Stock (page 72)

  ¼ teaspoon coltsfoot ash

  ¼ teaspoon black pepper, freshly ground

Combine oil and flour in a cold saucepan. Using a whisk, blend well.

Add Dark Game Stock gradually and whisk briskly until smoothly blended.

Stir over medium heat until thickened. Add coltsfoot ash and pepper.

WILD MUSTARD SAUCE

This recipe is based on the assumption that you will gather, dry, and grind wild mustard seeds. To do so, collect wild mustard seed pods as they are ripening and spread them on a screen over a sheet. When thoroughly dry, beat the pods to shake out the seeds. Grind the seeds to a fine powder and store in tightly sealed jars. Place a small slice of lemon in each jar and change these slices at least once a month. Use the dry mustard just as you would mustard powder. This recipe produces a hot mustard sauce. If you like it milder, add a little more olive oil.

¼   cup dry wild mustard powder

2   tablespoons Wild Herb Vinegar (page 68)

½   teaspoon olive oil

Place mustard powder in a small bowl. Add Wild Herb Vinegar and blend with a fork. Taste.

Add olive oil by drops and blend to desired consistency and taste.

WILD HORSERADISH SAUCE

This very pungent sauce is excellent, in moderation, on sliced game sandwiches or with deer or bear roasts.

1   small piece wild horseradish root

1   tablespoon Wild Herb Vinegar (page 68)

¾   cup yogurt

¼   teaspoon coltsfoot ash

Scrub, peel, and grate enough of the wild horseradish root to produce about 2 tablespoons of grates.

Place grated horseradish root in a bowl. Add Wild Herb Vinegar, stir, and let stand at room temperature 1 hour.

Press mixture and drain off any excess vinegar. Stir in yogurt and coltsfoot ash. Blend well.

Place sauce in a jar and cover tightly with a metal screw lid. Refrigerate until well chilled. Serve cold.

PAN GRAVY

Pan gravy is easily and quickly made from the pan juices left after frying or pan roasting or broiling any kind of small game, fish, or wildfowl. This basic recipe may be seasoned or spiced to complement the main dish.

   3 – 4   tablespoons pan juices

     2   tablespoons wild rice (*or* soy) flour

     1   cup stock (*or* water *or* milk), warmed

    ½   teaspoon coltsfoot ash

After cooking, remove all meat from the pan. If necessary, degrease the pan juices by touching with the edge of a rolled paper towel.

With heat very low, sprinkle flour over the pan juices. Use a whisk to blend thoroughly into a smooth paste.

Increase heat as you pour in about ½ of the warm liquid. Whisk to blend. Pour in remaining liquid and blend. Do not boil, but simmer rather strongly while stirring or whisking for about 5 minutes.

Add coltsfoot ash and other spices or seasonings that will complement main dish. Serve hot over steamed vegetables or cooked game or fish.

PARP'S ALL-PURPOSE SMALL-GAME SAUCE

This is a basic recipe and may be freely adapted: increased, spiced, or sweetened. It may be made with the pan juices or stock from any meat dish but is most delicious when made with the juices of red-meat small-game dishes.

½ cup warm pan juices (*or* stock)

3 tablespoons flour

1 cup yogurt

¼ cup fresh mushrooms, preferably chanterelles (*or* 1 tablespoon young leaves of plantain, torn)

honey (optional)

tamari soy sauce (optional)

Heat 3 tablespoons of the pan juices over medium heat.

Whisk in flour until smooth.

Slowly blend in the remaining pan juices. Cook gently 5 – 7 minutes.

Fold in yogurt, add mushrooms. Season to taste, or sweeten with honey. Tamari soy sauce is a fine addition. Heat before serving, but do not boil.

WILD RICE STUFFING

- 3 cups boiling water
- 1 cup boiling stock
- 1 whole wild onion

giblets (optional)

- 1 cup wild rice
- ⅓ cup corn oil
- 2 tablespoons cattail shoots, chopped
- ⅓ cup wild carrots, chopped
- ¼ cup wild celery stalks, chopped
- ¼ cup wild mushrooms, diced
- ¼ cup water chestnuts, sliced
- 1 tablespoon peppergrass seeds

Combine water, stock, and wild onion in a large pot. If giblets are available, chop them and add to boiling liquid and simmer 10 minutes.

Remove giblets and wild onion. Reserve giblets. Bring liquid to a full boil. Stir in wild rice so boiling does not stop. Reduce heat and simmer, uncovered, 30 minutes.

Heat corn oil in a skillet. Add cattail shoots, wild carrots, and wild celery. Sauté lightly.

Drain cooked wild rice. Add this and the giblets to the sautéed vegetables. Add mushrooms, water chestnuts, and peppergrass seeds. Stir to blend well, then use to stuff any wild or domestic fowl, or as a side dressing with any wild game.

WILD APPLE DRESSING

- 1 cup currants
- 6 cups soft bread crumbs
- ½ cup safflower oil
- 1 cup wild onions, chopped
- 1 cup wild celery stalks, chopped
- 1 clove garlic, minced
- 3 cups wild apples, diced
- ⅓ cup cattail shoots, chopped
- 1 teaspoon coltsfoot ash
- ¼ teaspoon paprika

Soak currants overnight in lukewarm water. Drain and place in boiling water for 10 minutes. Drain.

Combine bread crumbs and currants in a large bowl.

Heat safflower oil in a skillet and lightly sauté onions, celery, and garlic. Drain and combine with bread mixture.

Add remaining ingredients and toss together. Serve with venison or other big-game meat.

SAUCES, GRAVIES, AND STUFFINGS

WILD ONION STUFFING

- 2 cups wild onions, chopped
- 3 cups boiling water
- 3 cups stale bread crumbs
- 1 egg, beaten
- ¼ cup corn oil
- ½ teaspoon coltsfoot ash
- ⅛ teaspoon paprika
- ¼ teaspoon sage
- ⅛ teaspoon rosemary
- ⅛ teaspoon thyme
- ½ cup cattail shoots, chopped
- 1 cup Wildfowl Stock (page 74) (*or* Wild Vegetable Stock [page 77])

Combine wild onions and water in a large pot. Simmer 15 minutes. Drain and discard liquid.

Add all remaining ingredients except Wildfowl Stock. Use Wildfowl Stock to moisten mixture as needed. Use to stuff any wild or domestic fowl.

WILD MUSHROOM STUFFING

- ⅓ cup olive oil
- 1 cup wild mushrooms, chopped
- ¼ cup wild celery stalks, chopped
- ¼ cup wild caraway root, cooked and chopped

¼ cup wild onions, chopped

1 cup hot Wild Vegetable Stock (page 77)

3 cups stale bread crumbs

1 teaspoon coltsfoot ash

½ teaspoon sage

In a deep pot, heat olive oil and lightly sauté mushrooms, celery, caraway root, and onions. Add Wild Vegetable Stock and simmer 5 minutes.

Add bread crumbs, toss to moisten, and combine thoroughly. Sprinkle with coltsfoot ash and sage. Use to stuff any wild or domestic fowl.

YOGURT SAUCE FOR WILD VEGETABLES

This simple sauce is delicious served with cooked wild vegetables or as a dip for raw wild vegetables. The basic sauce may be varied by adding different seasonings and seeds.

1 cup yogurt

1 teaspoon wild caraway seeds

¼ teaspoon wild mint, chopped

⅛ teaspoon coltsfoot ash

Combine all ingredients except coltsfoot ash at least 2 hours before using. Refrigerate.

When ready to serve, stir in coltsfoot ash.

DRIED FRUIT AND NUT STUFFING

This is a special stuffing, excellent in all wild and domestic roast fowl. Use any dried fruit or berry that's available.

⅓ cup safflower oil

2 cups bread crumbs

2 cups dried fruit, chopped

1 cup cold water

¼ teaspoon spicebush

1 tablespoon honey

3 tablespoons lemon juice

¾ cup nuts, chopped

Place oil in a large saucepan over low heat. When warm, add bread crumbs and toss lightly to moisten.

In another saucepan, combine dried fruit, water, spicebush, honey, and lemon juice. Bring to a boil over high heat, then reduce heat to a very slow simmer for 10 minutes.

Combine fruit mixture with bread crumbs. Add chopped nuts and toss gently. Use while still warm and fresh to stuff your fowl.

WILD BARBECUE SAUCE

    2 tablespoons olive oil
    ¼ cup wild onions, chopped
    ½ cup water
    3 tablespoons Wild Herb Vinegar (page 68)
    1 tablespoon Wild Game Brown Sauce (page 104)
    3 tablespoons lemon juice
    1 cup Ground Cherry Sauce (page 102)
    2 tablespoons honey
    1 teaspoon watercress, chopped
    ½ teaspoon paprika

Heat olive oil in a heavy skillet. Add onions and sauté until browned.

Add remaining ingredients and stir. Simmer 30 minutes, stirring frequently.

CHAPTER SIX

SEAFOOD

What with oil spills and old tires, industrial waste and defense dumping, there is increasing concern over the safety of eating seafood. Very often, commercial crab and oysters are gathered in badly polluted or poisoned waters and can be quite dangerous, especially if eaten frequently or in excess. Parp advises extreme caution and temperance with regard to commercial seafood, especially shellfish.

But this book is dedicated to the individual wild foods gatherer and is not intended to apply to commercial goods. If you obtain your own seafood, and if you are alert to the presence of pollution, you should be able to avoid the worst dangers. Nevertheless, Parp suggests that no one should eat seafood, shellfish in particular, on an everyday basis.

SEAFOOD

RED SNAPPER BAKED WITH ORANGES

This recipe applies to any large fish. It is one of Parp's personal recipes developed in, of all places, Detroit.

        1   3-pound red snapper
    1½   cups Steamed Wild Rice (page 298) (*or* Wild Rice Stuffing [page 108])
        1   tablespoon safflower oil
        ½   teaspoon honey, warmed
        2   cups orange sections
        ¼   teaspoon paprika
        1   teaspoon warm water

Preheat oven to 350°F.

Prepare fish for baking. Wash and pat dry.

Place fish in oiled baking dish. Stuff with Steamed Wild Rice.

Brush fish with safflower oil and dot with honey.

Surround fish with orange sections and sprinkle with paprika.

Sprinkle the water around fish. Bake uncovered for 30 minutes, or to an internal temperature of 145°F. Serve from baking dish.

Yield: *4 – 6 servings*

FLOUNDER WITH MUSSEL SAUCE

1 tablespoon olive oil

2 tablespoons safflower oil

2 cloves garlic, minced

½ cup parsley, chopped

1 cup mussels, minced

¼ cup liquid from mussels (*or* clams)

2 pounds flounder fillets (6 – 8 fillets)

⅓ cup lemon juice

⅛ teaspoon cayenne pepper

Preheat oven to 350°F.

To make the mussel sauce, first combine oils and heat in a heavy skillet. Do not allow to smoke.

Add garlic. Cook over low heat for 3 – 4 minutes. Add parsley, mussels, and liquid. Simmer 10 minutes.

Place fillets in a shallow, oiled baking dish. Smother with mussel sauce.

Bake, uncovered, 30 minutes. Add lemon juice and cayenne. Serve with Steamed Wild Rice (page 298).

Yield: *6 servings*

SEAFOOD

HALIBUT ASPIC

   6 heads of halibut (*or* trout)

   6 cups cold water

  ¼ cup watercress, chopped

   1 teaspoon dill

  ¼ teaspoon coltsfoot ash

Place fish heads in water. Bring to a simmer and cook for 1 hour.

Strain the liquid into a mold or dish. Add watercress, dill, and coltsfoot ash.

Chill in refrigerator until set or use to prepare Poached Salmon (page 119).

Yield: *4 – 5 cups*

BAKED FILLETS OF FISH

6 – 8 small fillets of fish

   1 cup Mushroom Soup, warmed (page 82)

  ¼ cup yogurt

  ⅛ teaspoon cayenne pepper

Preheat oven to 350°F.

Place fish fillets in a baking dish. Cover with soup.

Drop yogurt into soup by spoonfuls. Sprinkle cayenne pepper on top.

Bake uncovered for 10 minutes. Serve with Steamed Wild Rice (page 298) and sautéed chantarelle mushrooms.

Yield: *4 – 6 servings*

POACHED SALMON

    6 cups water (*or* Halibut Aspic [page 118])
4 – 6 salmon steaks
    4 whole peppercorns
    1 tablespoon lemon juice
    1 bay leaf

Bring water to a boil. Reduce heat slightly.

Place salmon steaks in hot liquid. Carefully bring to a simmer, but do not allow liquid to boil again.

Add peppercorns, lemon juice, and bay leaf. Simmer for 10 minutes.

If using aspic, place the steaks in a dish, cover with aspic, and chill thoroughly before serving.

If using water, drain the steaks and serve with rice.

Yield: *4 – 6 servings*

SEAFOOD

BAKED UNSTUFFED FISH

    1 3- to 4-pound fish

    2 tablespoons olive oil

    1 tablespoon safflower oil

    ¼ teaspoon cayenne pepper

    ½ cup yogurt

Preheat oven to 325°F.

Place fish in baking dish. Brush with ½ of the combined oils.

Bake for 15 minutes, then brush with remaining oils, sprinkle with cayenne, and dot with yogurt. Return to oven.

Bake, uncovered, for an additional 15 minutes (for 3-pound fish). Serve with lemon slices.

Yield: 4 − 6 servings

BROILED SALMON STEAKS

This recipe is delicious cooked over the glowing coals.

    4 − 6 salmon steaks, ¾-inch thick

    4 − 6 teaspoons safflower oil

    ½ cup juniper berries

    1 teaspoon black pepper

    4 − 6 lemon wedges (optional)

Brush the steaks with ½ of the safflower oil.

Press berries into each side of each salmon steak.

Place steaks on a rack about 6 inches above the hot coals. Broil 3 minutes. Brush with additional oil. Turn steaks and broil another 5 minutes.

Season steaks with pepper and serve with lemon wedges and steamed wild vegetables.

Yield: *4 – 6 servings*

BOILED EEL STEW

6	cups water
1	boiled eel, cut into pieces
3	yellow onions, quartered
3 – 4	potatoes, cut in pieces
½	cup wild celery stalks, chopped
½	bay leaf
¼	teaspoon cayenne pepper
½	teaspoon honey

Place water in a stew pot and bring to a boil. Simmer.

Add eel, onions, potatoes, celery, bay leaf, and cayenne. Simmer until vegetables are tender, about 1 hour.

Reduce heat to stop simmer. Let stand 5 minutes over low heat. Ladle fat and scum from surface.

Stir in honey. Serve with corn bread.

Yield: *4 – 6 servings*

SEAFOOD

BAKED HALIBUT
WITH HERB SAUCE

- 1 2- to 3-pound halibut
- 4 tablespoons olive oil
- 1 tablespoon safflower oil
- ¼ teaspoon paprika
- ¼ cup spring onions, chopped
- 1 teaspoon parsley, chopped
- ½ teaspoon chives, chopped
- 1 tablespoon lemon juice

Preheat oven to 350°F.

Place halibut in a baking dish.

Combine 1 tablespoon of the olive oil with the safflower oil. Brush over halibut. Sprinkle with paprika.

Cover tightly and bake 20−30 minutes.

While the halibut is baking, heat the remaining 3 tablespoons of olive oil in a skillet. Add remaining ingredients and cook over low heat for 5 minutes.

Spoon over halibut and serve immediately.

Yield: *4 −6 servings*

BAKED STUFFED SEA BASS

2 tablespoons safflower oil

¼ cup wild onions, minced

⅛ teaspoon dill

2 cups Steamed Wild Rice (page 298)

1 3- to 4-pound bass (*or* other fish)

⅛ teaspoon cayenne pepper

Preheat oven to 350°F.

Heat 1 tablespoon of the oil in a heavy skillet. Heat onions and dill in oil but do not cook beyond heating.

Add heated onions and dill to steamed rice. Stuff fish and place in a baking dish. Pack the excess stuffing around the sides of the dish.

Brush fish with remaining oil. Sprinkle lightly with cayenne.

Bake for 30 minutes or to an internal temperature of 140°F.

Yield: *4 − 6 servings*

SEAFOOD

STEAMED HARD-SHELL CRAB

1 live crab per person

½ cup lemon juice

sauce or melted butter (optional)

Place living crabs in sink. Heat sufficient water (150°F) to pour over the crabs. Stun the crabs with a thorough rinsing of hot water.

In a large pot with a tight lid, place water to a depth of 1 inch. Bring the water to a rapid boil and place steamer rack in the pot.

Place stunned crabs on rack above steaming water. Be sure water does not touch crabs.

Pour lemon juice over crabs. Cover and steam over medium-high heat for 40 minutes.

Serve with a sauce or melted butter.

BROILED HARD-SHELL CRAB

1 pound fresh crab meat

2 tablespoons safflower oil

2 teaspoons chives, minced

¼ teaspoon paprika

1 lemon wedge

Preheat broiler.

Place drained crab on a broiler pan. Pour oil over crab meat and sprinkle on 1 teaspoon of the chives.

Place under hot broiler for 3 minutes. Turn. Add remaining oil and chives. Sprinkle with paprika.

Replace under broiler for 5 minutes, basting as necessary. Squeeze lemon juice sparingly over crab meat. Serve immediately.

Yield: *4 servings*

OYSTERS ON THE HALF SHELL

This civilized, traditional recipe is surely the finest way to experience oysters. It is a superb dish and is said to be conducive to love in the afternoon.

> 6 oysters per person
> 1 cup cracked ice per serving
> 2 – 3 lemon wedges per serving

Prechill serving dishes.

Scrub shells well with a stiff brush to avoid getting sand and dirt in the oysters.

Place 1 cup cracked ice in each cold serving dish.

Open and drain oysters but do not dry.

Arrange oysters and lemon wedges on cracked ice. Serve very cold with tall glasses of cold water.

SEAFOOD

SAUTÉED ABALONE

If your abalone is fresh, remove it from the shells and cut away the darkest meat. Tenderize by pounding.

- 1½ pounds abalone meat
-   1 cup rye flour
-   1 teaspoon cayenne pepper
-   3 eggs
-   6 tablespoons safflower oil
- 1½ cups bread crumbs, seasoned

Cut abalone against the grain into ½-inch-thick steaks.

Combine flour and cayenne in a bowl.

In another bowl, combine the eggs with ½ of the oil.

Place bread crumbs in a third bowl.

Lightly coat abalone steaks with flour mixture. Pat well.

Dip steaks in egg mixture, them immediately pass through bread crumbs. Sprinkle with additional crumbs to assure an even coating.

Heat remaining safflower oil in a heavy skillet over moderate heat. Sauté coated abalone steaks very lightly. Serve immediately.

Yield: *2 – 4 servings*

SAUTÉED FILLET
OF FISH WITH FRUIT

1 – 3 tablespoons safflower oil

1 or 2 fillets per person

1 grapefruit, sectioned

2 – 3 oranges, sectioned

lemon juice to taste

Heat safflower oil in skillet. Olive oil is more satisfactory for sautéing but affects the delicate flavor of fish.

Gently lay fillets, unbreaded, in hot (not smoking) oil. Sauté until flaky and tender. Do not overcook.

Serve with sections of grapefruit and oranges. Sprinkle a small amount of freshly squeezed lemon juice on the top.

CHAPTER SEVEN

FRESH-
WATER
FOOD

Of the North American freshwater fish, Parp, like many others, prefers the small varieties—trout, bluegills, and sunfish in particular. These little swimmers are as much fun to eat as they are to catch, and are easy to prepare.

Many people ignore the scales on small fish, especially trout, and Parp was previously of this persuasion. Parp's friend Ish Steward recently proved that trout skin really is better with the scales removed.

Parp's trout-cleaning method is first to kill the fish with a sharp blow to the head. Then he uses a small, very sharp, lock-blade knife to make a clean slit from the vent to the point of skin between the gills. He then severs the gills from the head and inserts a finger into the gills. With a steady pull, the viscera come free in one unit. Then a thumbnail scrapes up the central vein to push out the dark blood. It's as easy as that.

FRESH-
WATER
FOOD

TROUT ALMONDINE

When the snow is melting off the high Rockies, the sounds and smells of the spring runoff bring Parp out with line and hook to begin another season of wandering in camouflage along the banks of Willow Creek. These are the days when he is surest of bringing home a small catch of native mountain trout, firm and pink fleshed. This is the first trout recipe Parp will use this year, and the one he'll use the most.

4	tablespoons olive oil
¼	cup almonds, slivered
½	teaspoon paprika
1	tablespoon lemon juice
1	tablespoon parsley, chopped
½	teaspoon peppergrass seeds
4 – 6	brook (*or* native) trout

Heat 2 tablespoons of the olive oil in a small skillet or saucepan over medium-low heat.

Add almonds, paprika, lemon juice, and parsley. Sauté until almonds are lightly browned.

Heat remaining oil in a large skillet over medium heat. Sprinkle peppergrass seeds over trout.

Sauté trout in oil. When the first side is browned, 5−7 minutes, turn the trout and pour the almond mixture over it.

Continue cooking another 4−5 minutes or until trout is done. Serve with Steamed Wild Rice (page 298) and fresh wild fruit.

Yield: 2−4 servings

BROILED TROUT

Per person:

2 tablespoons olive oil

1 teaspoon lemon juice

⅛ teaspoon paprika

1 whole trout, cleaned

lemon wedges (optional)

Preheat broiler.

Combine oil, lemon juice, and paprika. Brush each trout with this mixture and immediately place on a broiler pan.

Place trout under hot broiler for 6−7 minutes for a medium-size trout.

The trout is done when the flesh flakes easily but is still very moist. Do not overcook. Serve with lemon wedges, steamed rice, and fruit.

FRESH-
WATER
FOOD

TROUT IN YOGURT SAUCE

Here is a recipe you might try toward the end of the season, when you're beginning to think you never want to see another trout.

2 – 4 trout
1 – 2 tablespoons lemon juice
½ cup rye flour
4 tablespoons olive oil
1 cup yogurt
½ teaspoon Wild Herb Vinegar (page 68)
¼ teaspoon cayenne pepper
1 teaspoon honey

Brush the inside of each trout with lemon juice. Shake each trout in a paper sack of flour.

Heat 2 tablespoons of the olive oil in a heavy skillet. Sauté the trout until golden brown, about 7 minutes on each side.

When done, remove the trout to a platter or warming oven and keep hot.

To make sauce, add remaining oil to skillet and heat while scraping the pan. Gradually stir in yogurt. Cook over medium heat for 5 minutes but do not boil.

Blend in Wild Herb Vinegar, cayenne, and honey. Simmer together for another 5 minutes.

Serve trout with Steamed Wild Rice (page 298). Pour yogurt sauce on top.

Yield: *2 — 4 servings*

TROUT LOUIS

- 5 large lettuce leaves
- 1 cup lettuce, shredded
- 3 cups cold trout meat, boned
- 3 eggs, hard-boiled and sliced
- 1 lemon, cut in wedges (optional)
- 1 tablespoon chives, chopped

Line the inside of a large wooden salad bowl with the lettuce leaves.

Spread shredded lettuce evenly over the lettuce leaves.

Place trout meat on shredded lettuce covered with eggs. Squeeze 1 wedge of lemon over the trout.

Sprinkle chives over all. Serve in salad bowls with lemon wedges and, if you like, a light dressing.

Yield: *4 servings*

FRESH-
WATER
FOOD

TROUT AND EGGS

Parp likes to carry eggs in his pack for that first-day breakfast at the tipi. Every once in a while he'll also have tiny brook trout caught fresh that morning. Needless to say, he always carries parsley, but if fresh watercress is available he uses that instead.

4 tablespoons oil

4 – 6 small brook trout

2 eggs

1 tablespoon water

7 – 8 sprigs parsley (*or* watercress)

1 lemon

Heat 2 tablespoons of the oil in a heavy skillet. Get it as hot as possible without causing it to smoke.

Place trout in hot oil. Sauté 3 or 4 minutes or until very lightly browned.

Turn trout. Sauté another 3 minutes. Remove pan from heat. Remove trout to a warm pan near the fire.

Allow skillet to cool slightly. Add remaining oil and heat to medium. Crack eggs into oil so the yolks don't break. Add water and cover the pan. Cook near the fire's edge until done, about 3 minutes.

Slip cooked eggs out of pan and onto the trout. Garnish with ample parsley. Use lemon to season both eggs and fish. Devour, and hike your heart out all day long.

Yield: *1 – 2 servings*

TROUT OMELET

- 3 eggs
- 1 tablespoon water
- ½ teaspoon lemon juice
- 1 tablespoon safflower oil
- ½ cup cold trout meat, flaked
- ¼ cup cheddar cheese, shredded

Combine eggs, water, and lemon juice. Do not over-blend. Eggs should be streaked.

Heat oil in a medium-size skillet with flared sides, or in an omelet pan. Be sure oil covers the sides and bottom of the skillet.

Add omelet mixture. Before the bottom sets, use a fork to agitate the surface of the mixture. Keep the omelet loose by rapidly moving the skillet in circles. Cook for 3 minutes over medium heat.

When the omelet is set, remove the skillet from the heat. Add trout meat in very small flakes. Add cheese. Using a spatula, fold the omelet in half carefully, to cover the trout and cheese. Keep warm in 200°F oven to heat the trout and melt the cheese without overcooking the omelet. Serve immediately.

Yield: *2 – 3 servings*

FRESH-
WATER
FOOD

TROUT ORMSBY

This recipe is named for an old friend of Parp's, a man who appreciates fresh mountain trout as much as he appreciates good water and clean air. Fortunately, Ormsby lives in Parp's old stomping grounds, the San Juan Mountains, where the trout are plentiful. It's a good thing, for poor Ormsby cannot get through one entire day without his trout. Every day, about 3:00 P.M., Ormsby's eyes glaze over and he starts to blubber. When he starts turning over rocks, his friends all know that it's time for his fish. Here's his method of cooking fresh mountain trout.

> 1 or 2 fresh trout
>
> wild mushrooms
>
> butter
>
> pepper

Build a good fire to deep, glowing coals.

Find a thin, oval-shaped rock.

Place the rock in the fire to heat thoroughly.

Stuff 1 or 2 cleaned, fresh trout with wild mushrooms, butter, and pepper. Some say onions. Wrap stuffed trout in foil or in the large leaves of any nontoxic plant or shrub.

Place wrapped trout on a hot rock and allow to bake.

Trout is ready to eat when foil turns brown or leaves begin to burn. Eat without utensils.

CAMPFIRE TROUT

We call this Campfire Trout, but Picnic Trout might be a better name. The recipe depends on aluminum foil and even Parp doesn't carry foil in his pack. But for one of those days at the hot springs with the whole gang, this is Parp's choice outdoor trout recipe.

Per person:

1	tablespoon safflower oil
1	teaspoon lemon juice
⅛	teaspoon peppergrass seeds
1 or 2	fresh trout
¼	cup yogurt
¼	cup chantarelles (*or* other wild mushrooms)

black olives, sliced (optional)

nuts (optional)

Let the campfire burn down to glowing coals. Combine oil, lemon juice, and peppergrass seeds. Brush each trout with this mixture.

Combine yogurt and mushrooms.

Partially wrap a trout with foil, cavity up, to form a pouch. Fill the cavity with yogurt and mushrooms and allow to overflow onto the sides of the fish. You may also wish to add sliced black olives or nuts.

Wrap fish, but not too tightly. Place 6–8 inches above hot coals. Do not turn. When the foil becomes slightly browned, trout is done. Do not overcook.

FRESH-WATER FOOD

SIMPLE CAMPFIRE TROUT

Parp has savored this simple meal again and again. It has the magic of ritual and the romance of the individual living in the wilderness as naturally as his fellow creatures. Nothing is better at dawn or at dusk.

    1 or 2 brook trout per person

Clean the trout, leaving head and tail on, of course.

Impale the trout on a cleaned stick.

Hold the trout just outside of the flames of your fire, or over coals. Heat thoroughly but do not overcook. No seasonings or utensils should be necessary.

BOILED CRAYFISH

Here's another special dish from the Midwest. Like carp, crayfish should be kept alive in cold running water for at least 3 or 4 days, then cooked alive.

    2 quarts water

    1 leek

    1 teaspoon parsley, chopped

    1 carrot, chopped

    ¼ teaspoon cayenne pepper

10 – 12 crayfish per person

melted butter (optional)

Bring water to a full boil. Add leek, parsley, carrot, and cayenne pepper.

Drop crayfish into the boiling water, 1 or 2 at a time. Do not allow boiling to slow. Boil until they turn bright red.

Serve with melted butter. Break the center tail fin to remove intestines, if desired. Peel and eat without utensils.

BAKED FRESH BASS

    1 2-pound bass
    2 tablespoons olive oil
    ¼ teaspoon paprika
    ⅛ teaspoon nutmeg
    1 tablespoon lemon juice
    1 lemon, cut in wedges (optional)

Preheat oven to 350°F. Place fish in baking dish.

Combine oil, paprika, and nutmeg. Brush this mixture generously over the bass.

Cover tightly and bake for 20 minutes.

Remove from oven and immediately sprinkle with the lemon juice. Serve with lemon wedges and steamed vegetables.

Yield: *2 − 4 servings*

SAUTÉED FROG LEGS

   1 egg

  ½ cup cornmeal

  ¼ teaspoon peppergrass seeds

  2 pounds frog legs

  ½ cup safflower oil

  1 lemon, cut in wedges (optional)

Partially beat the egg. Combine with cornmeal and peppergrass seeds to make a batter.

Coat each frog leg by dipping it into the batter.

Heat oil in a large skillet over medium-high heat. Do not allow oil to smoke.

Carefully place frog legs in hot oil. Sauté 20 minutes, turning once to brown all sides. Serve legs with lemon.

Yield: 2 − 4 servings

BAKED CARP

Do not eat a carp that dies soon after being caught. Bring your carp home alive and keep it alive in your bathtub for at least 3 or 4 days. Change the water twice each day by removing the drain plug and running in more fresh, cold water than is draining out. Never kill a carp until you are ready to eat it.

   1 3- to 4-pound living carp

   ¼ cup corn oil

   2 lemons, cut in wedges (optional)

   sprigs of parsley (optional)

Preheat oven to 325°F.

Kill the carp by hitting it in the head with the back of a heavy knife. Clean by slitting the belly. Rinse. Slit the skin along the back with 2 or 3 knife gashes.

Place carp on a well-oiled, very shallow baking dish. Brush with oil.

Bake to an internal temperature of 150°F, about 30 minutes. Serve with lemon wedges and parsley.

Yield: *3 — 4 servings*

WHITEFISH IN CREAM SAUCE

    3 tablespoons safflower oil
    4 tablespoons wild rice flour
 1½ cups skim milk
    3 whole cloves
    1 wild onion
    1 bay leaf
    1 teaspoon fresh dill, chopped
  ¼ teaspoon coltsfoot ash
    4 fillets of whitefish
    1 tablespoon parsley, chopped

Preheat oven to 350°F.

Place oil in a casserole dish over low heat. Add flour and stir with a whisk while cooking for about 3 minutes.

Gradually add the milk while whisking slowly.

Push the cloves into the onion. Place onion in sauce. Add bay leaf. Cook and whisk until the mixture thickens. Add dill and coltsfoot ash.

Place fillets of whitefish in a large casserole dish. Cover with cream sauce and bake to an internal temperature of 145°F, about 25 minutes.

Sprinkle with parsley and serve immediately.

Yield: *4 servings*

FRESH-
WATER
FOOD

PAN-FRIED SUNFISH

6 – 8 sunfish (*or* other small pan fish)

2 eggs, beaten

1 cup cornmeal, seasoned

3 tablespoons corn oil

lemon juice

1 lemon, cut in wedges (optional)

Fish should be cleaned, whole, and at room temperature.

Slide each fish through the beaten eggs, then roll in cornmeal spread on a platter.

Heat oil in a heavy skillet. Get the oil as hot as possible without causing it to smoke. Squeeze in a few drops of lemon juice. Place the fish in the hot oil. Reduce heat somewhat.

When the fish is browned on one side, about 3 or 4 minutes, turn and fry the other side. Sprinkle with lemon juice. Remove from heat and serve immediately with lemon wedges and hash browns, steamed rice, or wild vegetables.

Yield: *2 – 4 servings*

SOUTHERN FRIED CATFISH

This is adapted from the traditional Southern recipe, a recipe that is as popular in southern Illinois as it is in Mississippi.

    corn oil
    ½ teaspoon peppergrass seeds
    1 cup white cornmeal
    1 catfish, cleaned and skinned
    ½ teaspoon lemon juice

Add oil to deep fryer and heat to 370°F.

Combine peppergrass seeds and cornmeal. Coat catfish with seasoned cornmeal.

Immerse catfish in deep fryer. Fry until lightly browned.

Remove catfish from fryer. Sprinkle with lemon juice. Serve immediately with sliced tomatoes and green beans.

Yield: *2 servings*

CHAPTER EIGHT

NORTH AMERICAN WILDFOWL

Most people who've eaten from the woods for any extended period of time agree that red meat grows rather tiresome in the course of a long winter. Old trappers, hunters, and other experienced woodspeople treasure fine birds above all other dietary treats. Elk, deer, rabbit, and squirrel may fill the freezer or the larder, but they alone cannot satisfy the appetites of wilderness people for long. Quail, pheasant, turkey, ptarmigan—these are also necessities if you prefer not to starve from boredom. Indeed, many woodspeople much prefer fine wildfowl to any other food. In our San Juan Mountains, certainly, there is nothing better than our native grouse.

Many hunters are rather cavalier in their field treatment of freshly killed game birds. The common belief that birds will keep, uncleaned, for a day or two is simply not true. Even on a cold day the meat can easily be tainted by intestines. Game birds should always be cleaned immediately after the kill.

The easiest way to clean a bird is first to pluck it partially from the breastbone to the vent. Then, using a small, sharp knife, slit the skin and membrane around the vent and up to the breastbone. Be careful not to pierce the intestines or stomach. Next reach one hand up through the breast cavity into the neck, loosen the windpipe and pull out the whole system from the windpipe to the intestines. If the contents of the intestines or stomach touch any part of the meat, that part should be cut away and discarded. Many hunters then fill the cavity with snow, cool grass, or spruce boughs.

All game birds should be dry-plucked, never scalded. First hang the drawn bird for a period of 24 to 48 hours at 40°F, then pluck it by pulling the feathers down in the direction in which they grow. Take care not to tear the skin, which is very thin and delicate. After a brief hanging, plucked birds may be cooked, frozen, or canned.

147

NORTH
AMERICAN
WILDFOWL

BRAISED GAME BIRDS

Here's another recipe designed to reduce the toughest and oldest game birds to tender, succulent meat. Whenever Parp comes home with an odd assortment of birds, this is how he prepares them.

2	tablespoons olive oil
2 – 3	pounds game birds, cut in pieces
1	cup Wildfowl Stock, cooled slightly from boiling (page 74)
¼	cup wild onions, sautéed and chopped
2	tablespoons honey
¼	teaspoon rosemary
½	cup yogurt
2	tablespoons flour
¼	cup milk

pepper to taste

Preheat oven to 325°F.

Heat olive oil in a heavy skillet, 1 tablespoon at a time, and lightly brown the game bird pieces.

Place the browned pieces in a baking dish.

Add Wildfowl Stock, sautéed onions, and honey. Sprinkle rosemary on top.

Cover and bake for 1 hour. Remove cover and add yogurt by the spoonful. Return to oven and bake, uncovered, an additional 20 minutes.

Remove meat from baking dish. Blend flour and milk in a jar. Blend this mixture into the pan liquid. Simmer over moderate heat for 5 minutes. Pour sauce over meat and serve with Steamed Wild Rice (page 298).

Yield: *4 servings*

ROAST PHEASANT

Only young pheasants should be roasted. The young bird has gray legs and long pointed feathers in its wings. After it is drawn and plucked, its breast bone will remain soft and flexible. Such a pheasant should be hung for 48 hours, first by one leg, then the other. Older pheasants should be used in stews, for stock, or canned in liquid.

1 **young pheasant**
4 **cups Wild Rice Stuffing (page 108)**

Preheat oven to 400°F.

Stuff the pheasant and place in large, uncovered roasting pan.

Place in oven and immediately reduce heat to 325°F and roast for about 3 hours.

Yield: *2 servings*

PHEASANT IN YOGURT
WITH WILD RICE

This is the best recipe for older, tougher pheasants. The moist heat and slow cooking will tenderize and flavor the meat thoroughly.

1 pheasant

¼ teaspoon tarragon

½ teaspoon coltsfoot ash

2 tablespoons corn oil

1 tangerine (*or* lemon), quartered

1 cup yogurt

1 tablespoon warm water

Preheat oven to 300°F.

Cut pheasant into serving pieces. Reserve wings and back for stock.

Cover pheasant with hot water and simmer for 20 minutes.

Remove pheasant from water and pat dry with a clean cloth. Sprinkle with tarragon and coltsfoot ash.

Heat corn oil in a heavy casserole. Lightly brown pheasant pieces in oil.

Remove casserole from heat. Squeeze tangerine juice over the meat.

Add the yogurt and the tablespoon of warm water. Cover and bake for 2 hours. Serve with Steamed Wild Rice (page 298).

Yield: *2 servings*

BROILED PHEASANT

This is how Parp prepares fowl. It is especially delicious with young pheasant.

- 1 pheasant
- ¼ cup corn oil
- ¼ teaspoon tarragon
- 1 tangerine, quartered

Split pheasant in half, lengthways. Use a small amount of the corn oil to lightly cover the bottom of a broiler pan.

Place pheasant in broiler pan, skin side down. Sprinkle with tarragon.

Place under broiler for 10 minutes.

Turn pheasant halves. Add remaining corn oil. Squeeze tangerine over pheasant.

Return to broiler for 10 – 15 minutes, basting often. The pheasant is ready when its juices run clear from a knife-point puncture.

Yield: *2 servings*

GAME BIRD STEW

This recipe is suitable for most game birds. Make sure the stew doesn't boil while the meat is in the liquid.

- 5 – 7 pounds game birds, cut in pieces
- 1 quart water (*or* stock), cooled slightly from boiling
- 3 wild celery stalks, cut in long pieces
- 1½ wild onions, sliced
- 1½ cups fresh garden peas (*or* chopped daylily buds)
- 2 tablespoons peppergrass seeds
- 1 dash cayenne pepper
- 1 teaspoon coltsfoot ash
- 1 teaspoon lemon juice
- 2 tablespoons flour
- ¼ cup cold water

Place game bird pieces in a stew pot with the water.

Add wild celery and wild onions.

Stew slowly for 1 hour and remove scum from surface.

Add peas, peppergrass seeds, cayenne, coltsfoot ash, and lemon juice at the end of the first hour. Continue to simmer for another hour. Do not allow to boil.

Remove meat and vegetables from stock and keep warm. Bring the stock to a rapid boil. Boil for 20 minutes. Strain.

Place flour in a small screw-top jar. Add cold water, cover, and shake to blend thoroughly. Slowly pour this mixture into the stock while stirring. Cook over moderate heat to thicken as desired. Return solid food to thickened stock and serve over steamed rice.

Yield: *6 servings*

GLAZED DUCK

1	whole duck
1	clove garlic
3	wild celery stalks
2	wild onions, sliced
1½	cups orange sections
½	cup honey

Preheat oven to 400°F.

Prepare the duck for roasting. Rub with garlic and place on a rack in a roasting pan.

Fill body cavity with wild celery and onions.

Place duck, uncovered, in oven. Immediately reduce the heat to 325°F. Roast 45 minutes, until almost done.

Press orange sections until quite pulpy. Combine with honey. Remove duck and increase oven heat to 450°F.

Cover duck with orange/honey glaze. Place in hot oven 20 minutes, or until duck is glazed and done.

Yield: *2 servings*

NORTH
AMERICAN
WILDFOWL

ROAST WILD DUCK

- 2 young wild ducks at room temperature
- ¼ cup corn oil
- 2 wild onions, quartered
- 1 wild apple, cored, peeled, and sliced
- ¼ cup wild apple juice
- ¼ cup rose hips (*or* dried violet flowers)
- 1 cup yogurt

Preheat oven to 475°F.

Rub ducks inside and out with corn oil.

Loosely fill the cavities with pieces of onion and apple.

Place ducks on a rack in a roasting pan. Place, uncovered, in oven.

Immediately reduce oven heat to 375°F and roast 20 minutes.

Remove ducks from pan. Strain and degrease the drippings. Remove and discard onion and apple pieces. Add apple juice and rose hips to drippings in roasting pan. Simmer 20 minutes, stirring occasionally.

Blend in yogurt over low heat and bring almost to a simmer. Pour this sauce over the 2 ducks.

Serve with Steamed Wild Rice (page 298), wild fruit, and nuts.

Yield: *4 servings*

BROILED DUCK

1 or 2 young ducks

¼ cup corn oil

½ teaspoon paprika

¼ cup clear, unseasoned fowl stock

½ lemon

2 oranges, sectioned

yogurt (enough to thicken)

Preheat broiler.

Split each duck down the back and spread in broiler pan.

Brush duck skin with corn oil. Sprinkle with paprika.

Place under hot broiler, 4—6 inches from the heat. Baste frequently with stock.

After 15 minutes, squeeze lemon juice over ducks.

When almost done (about another 5 minutes), distribute oranges over ducks. Return to broiler for 5 minutes.

Remove ducks and fruit pieces. Use the drippings to make a sauce thickened with yogurt. Serve with Steamed Wild Rice (page 298) and stuffed apples.

Yield: *2 —4 servings*

NORTH
AMERICAN
WILDFOWL

ROAST WILD TURKEY

The wild turkey is certainly one of the most difficult of all creatures to obtain and challenges the skill of even the best hunters. No one can simply pick up a shotgun, walk into a field, and bring home a turkey. A hunter may spend months watching, stalking, and preparing for the final day, the hunt itself. The turkey is an exceedingly wary bird, superbly camouflaged, silent as a leaf falling, and equipped with finely tuned senses. Very few hunters ever see a wild turkey, even if they spend their lives in a prime turkey area. Compared to a wild turkey, a black bear is a rabbitlike pushover.

But if you do get a wild turkey, especially a young one, you can look forward to an incomparable feast. A turkey should be drawn immediately after the kill and then hung for 7 days. Dry pluck the bird after hanging and do not singe or wash. Wild turkey should be roasted with plenty of moisture, whether young or old. Remember that the meat of the wings and legs is much denser than the breast or back meat. The breast meat will, therefore, cook much faster than the legs or wings and must be protected against overcooking until the legs are tender. Be sure to use a cooking cloth soaked in corn oil for this purpose. Overcooking a wild turkey is a terrible sin against nature.

Prepare your turkey for roasting by this method.

Place a rack large enough for your bird in a large roasting pan that has a tight cover.

Pour in hot water to within ¼ inch of the rack. Place the turkey on the rack. Be sure that no part of the turkey touches water.

Steam for 45 minutes over low to moderate heat—just enough to produce adequate steam without splashing hot water over the turkey. Do not prick the bird or puncture with a knife.

Remove the turkey from the roasting pan and allow to cool to room temperature. This won't take long as the steaming should not have heated the bird to the point of cooking. You are now ready to begin the roasting procedure.

1 turkey, prepared as above

corn oil

Wild Rice Stuffing (page 108)
    (or Wild Apple Dressing [page 109]
    or Wild Mushroom Stuffing [page 110])

1 cooking cloth, soaked with corn oil

Stuff turkey.

Brush turkey with corn oil. Roast, uncovered in 375°F oven, until lightly browned.

Cover breast with a cooking cloth soaked with corn oil. Reduce oven heat to 325°F and roast until tender, allowing 15 minutes per pound. Baste often with additional corn oil.

Remove cooking cloth for the last 20 minutes. Allow turkey to cool for about 10 minutes before carving. Do not remove from roasting pan until ready to serve.

Yield: *4 – 6 servings*

BROILED QUAIL

If the fat on your quail is firm but not hard, you can
broil it with satisfactory results. If hard fat indicates an
older bird, however, then a recipe like Baked Breast of
Quail (page 160) will provide a better meal.

  2 – 4 quail

    1 teaspoon peppergrass seeds

    ½ teaspoon thyme

    ¼ cup corn oil (*or* olive oil)

    1 lemon, quartered

Preheat broiler.

Split quail down the back. Sprinkle with peppergrass
seeds and thyme.

Place skin side down in broiler pan. Lightly coat with
oil.

Place under hot broiler until underside is lightly
browned, about 10 minutes.

Turn skin side up. Squeeze lemon juice liberally onto
skins. Continue broiling and basting with hot oil until
tender. Do not overbroil. Serve with steamed wild vegetables or baked potatoes and carrots.

Yield: *2 servings*

SMOTHERED QUAIL

  2 quail, cut in pieces

  ½ cup rye flour

  ¼ cup olive oil

  1 large onion, sliced

  1 clove garlic, chopped

  3 celery stalks, cut in long pieces

  2 carrots, cut in long pieces

1½ cups Wildfowl Stock (page 74)

  1 cup mushrooms, sliced

  ½ cup black olives, sliced

Preheat oven to 325°F.

Place quail pieces, 3 or 4 at a time, in a paper sack with rye flour. Shake to coat all pieces.

Heat olive oil to 375°F in a skillet. Brown coated quail.

Place browned quail pieces in a casserole dish.

Sauté onion, garlic, celery, and carrots in the hot olive oil for 7 minutes.

Drain vegetables and distribute over quail pieces, then pour the Wildlife Stock on top.

Bake, uncovered, for 1½ hours. Ten minutes before done, add mushrooms and olives.

Yield: *2 – 4 servings*

BAKED BREAST OF QUAIL

Quail wings and legs are best used for stock, if at all.
They are much tougher than the breast meat, even in
the youngest birds, and mainly consist of tendons and
inedible membrane. Many people use the wings and
legs for pet food, to avoid waste, and prepare only the
breasts for the table.

2 – 4 quail breasts, carefully cleaned

1 teaspoon coltsfoot ash

1 teaspoon tarragon

2 tablespoons lemon juice

2 teaspoons tamari soy sauce

⅓ cup Wild Herb Vinegar (page 68)

2 yellow onions, quartered

⅓ cup Wildfowl Stock (page 74) (*or* Wild
Vegetable Stock [page 77]

1 cup yogurt

2 tablespoons parsley

Preheat oven to 400°F.

Gently rub quail with coltsfoot ash and tarragon. Place
in a heavy, shallow baking pan.

Sprinkle quail with lemon juice, soy sauce, and Wild
Herb Vinegar. Surround with onion pieces.

Bake for 10 minutes. Reduce heat to 350°F. Cover and
bake for 30 minutes, basting twice in that time.

Remove cover and bake an additional 15 minutes.

Remove from oven and move quail to a warming oven or heated platter.

In a saucepan, combine Wildfowl Stock with juice from the baking pan. Simmer over low heat for 3 – 4 minutes. Add yogurt.

Cover quail with yogurt sauce. Sprinkle with parsley. Serve with Steamed Wild Rice (page 298).

Yield: *2 servings*

ROAST WILD GOOSE

Again, only young birds should be roasted. Others should be cut up and braised or smothered. Proper preparation of the bird for roasting is most important. Geese should always be drawn immediately after the kill. Wild geese do not have the high fat and grease content of the domestic variety and must be roasted differently.

Remove the goose from the refrigerator 24 hours before you plan to begin roasting.

Place a cored and peeled apple, a quartered onion, and a sliced potato in the chest cavity of the goose.

The goose should sit in an airy place at room temperature for 20 hours with the vegetables inside. Then preheat oven to 400°F. Cook goose for 15 minutes.

Remove goose from oven. Remove and discard vegetables. Your bird is now ready to stuff and roast.

1 young goose, prepared as above

2 tablespoons lemon juice

1 tablespoon peppergrass seeds

4 cups Wild Rice Stuffing (page 108)

1 cooking cloth, soaked with corn oil

1 cup Wildfowl Stock (page 74)

Preheat oven to 300°F.

Rub the prepared goose with combined lemon juice and peppergrass seeds.

Stuff with Wild Rice Stuffing and truss.

Cover breast with cooking cloth soaked with corn oil.

Place, uncovered, on a rack in a roasting pan. Roast 20 minutes to the pound. Add stock as necessary to retain moisture.

When the leg joints move easily, increase oven temperature to 375°F and remove the cooking cloth. Allow the breast to brown at this temperature, about 20 minutes.

Serve with stuffing, cabbage, caraway root, and fruit.

Yield: *4 – 6 servings*

ROAST GROUSE IN ORANGE SAUCE

This recipe is ideal for older grouse. The slow cooking in moist heat tenderizes the meat, while basting with the orange juice creates a wonderful flavor.

2 – 4	whole breasts of grouse
4	tablespoons corn oil
1 or 2	oranges, juiced
1	tablespoon watercress, chopped
½	teaspoon coltsfoot ash
¼	cup warm water

Preheat oven to 375°F.

Split the grouse down the backbone (legs and wings removed) and flatten without separating.

Heat 1 tablespoon of the corn oil in a heavy skillet. Very lightly brown the skin on the meaty sides of the breasts.

Remove breasts from skillet and brush both sides with the remaining corn oil.

Place bony side up in roasting pan. Roast, uncovered, for 20 minutes.

Remove from oven and turn breasts meaty side up. Reduce oven heat to 300°F. Pour orange juice over breasts. Add watercress. Cover, return to oven, and roast for 45 minutes, basting twice.

Remove from oven and sprinkle with coltsfoot ash. Add warm water around sides to increase moisture as needed. Return to oven and roast, uncovered, an additional 20 minutes, basting once.

Remove grouse from roasting pan and place on serving platter. Pour pan juices over the grouse. Serve with sweet potatoes and cranberry sauce.

Yield: *2 – 4 servings*

ROAST PARTRIDGE

Allow 1 young partridge per person. A partridge is young if its first flight feather is pointed. Older birds should be braised. The partridge is a very dry bird and care must be taken to allow ample moisture. One good approach is to simmer the bird in a combination of stock and lemon juice before roasting. This both adds moisture to the meat and reduces the roasting time.

    2–4 partridges
      1 cup corn oil
      ½ teaspoon black pepper
      1 onion, quartered
      1 apple, quartered
    2–4 cooking cloths, soaked with corn oil
      ¼ cup hot water

Preheat oven to 375°F.

Brush each partridge with corn oil and sprinkle with black pepper.

Place onion and apple pieces in each partridge.

Place partridge in roasting pan and place in oven. Immediately reduce heat to 300°F and roast until lightly browned, about 15 minutes.

Cover each partridge with a cooking cloth soaked with corn oil. Add the hot water, poured around sides.

Cover and continue to roast for 45 minutes or until tender. Baste often and add more corn oil as necessary.

Remove cooking cloths for the last 10 minutes.

When done, discard onion and apple pieces. Serve with pan gravy and boiled potatoes.

Yield: 2 − 4 servings

BROILED GROUSE

As with other game birds, only young grouse should be broiled. All others should be cooked by a moist-heat process. Again, use only the breast of the grouse and reserve the wings and legs for stock.

- 2 − 4 **whole breasts of grouse**
- 1 − 3 **tablespoons corn oil**
-   ½ **teaspoon black pepper, freshly ground**
-   1 **tablespoon lemon juice**

Preheat broiler.

Split the grouse (wings and legs removed) down the backbone and flatten without separating.

Brush both sides with corn oil. Sprinkle with pepper.

Place breasts meat-side-down in broiler pan. Place under hot broiler for 7 minutes.

Turn breasts meat-side-up and sprinkle with lemon juice. Return to broiler for 7 minutes.

Serve with berries and Steamed Wild Rice (page 298).

Yield: 2 − 4 servings

NORTH
AMERICAN
WILDFOWL

GROUSE CASSEROLE SUPREME

This dish may also be prepared using the breasts of quail, duck, or pheasant. A variation on the standard French casserole recipe, it has long been a favorite with Parp and his friends.

3	tablespoons olive oil
2 – 4	breasts of grouse
¼	cup apple cider vinegar
2	wild apples, cored and sliced
½	orange, sectioned
1	cup wild celery stalks, chopped
1	wild onion, chopped
3 or 4	sprigs watercress
½	teaspoon lemon juice
¼	teaspoon paprika
3	tablespoons flour
2	cups Wildfowl Stock (page 74) (*or* Wild Vegetable Stock [page 77])
½	cup yogurt
1	teaspoon tarragon
1	cup Parmesan cheese, grated

Heat olive oil in a large, heavy skillet that has a close-fitting cover. Brown breast meat on both sides. Pour vinegar over meat.

Lower heat to simmer and remove breasts. Add apples, orange sections, celery, onion, watercress, lemon juice, and paprika. Cover and cook over low heat for 20 minutes.

Add flour and blend in with a wire whisk. Add Wildfowl Stock and increase heat. Stir and cook to boiling point. Lower heat.

Return breasts to sauce. Cover and simmer until tender, about 1 hour.

Remove breasts to a shallow baking dish. Strain sauce and keep hot while adding yogurt and tarragon. Blend well with whisk.

Pour sauce over breasts in baking dish. Sprinkle Parmesan cheese on the top.

Place dish under broiler, though not too close. Allow cheese to brown slightly around the edges.

Yield: *2 − 4 servings*

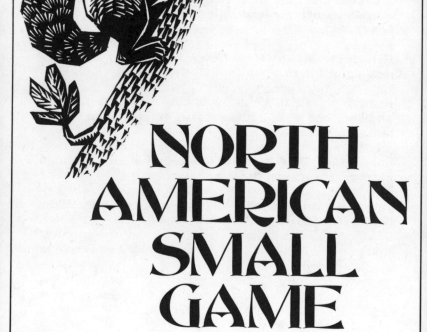

CHAPTER NINE

NORTH AMERICAN SMALL GAME

You will need a .22 caliber rifle or a good bow and arrow, or maybe a light shotgun. You'll also need a small sharp knife, a small scissors, rubber gloves, a container of disinfectant, some string, and a game bag or shoulder pack.

Parp prefers the .22 and will shoot at an animal only when he is certain of hitting it square in the head—killing cleanly, instantly, and with minimum damage. Parp is also superstitious and will shoot an animal only when he feels right about it. This is no doubt a residual form of the primitive belief that the hunted animal is ready to die and offers its flesh as food for the living, who will do likewise later.

We would like to assert, before we go any further, that hunting, by itself, is not a threat to the small game of North America. The threats to small game are pollution (including herbicides and pesticides), and reduced habitat. One should, of course, use sensitive judgement about hunting in any area where these or other threats are already present. Killing the last gray squirrel in a Georgia woodlot would be quite comparable to force feeding marshmallows to the last grizzly in Wyoming. On the other hand, thinning the squirrel population in a large oak forest near a farming community can only be good for the forest, the farmers, and your stew pot. There are many factors which we must consider in order to be responsible wild food gatherers. We are not advocating that everyone in New York City go kill a

rabbit in Connecticut. We are asserting that anyone who reads this far in this book can go someplace and get some kind of small game without endangering the balance of nature.

All small animals intended for the table require thorough and immediate cleaning in order to avoid tainted or excessively gamey meat.

The next section of this book discusses field care of small-game animals. Note that the fat of all small-game animals turns rancid very quickly and should never be preserved or used for cooking. It should always be completely removed from the meat and discarded.

Also note that many critters come supplied with small glands that may be under the front legs, along the small of the back, or both. These glands and their contents will ruin any meat they touch and, if not removed, will make the cooked meat unpalatable. Whenever you remove the glands from an animal be sure to clean your knife thoroughly afterward. A knife so contaminated will in turn contaminate any meat it touches.

Parp says he never wears rubber gloves when cleaning animals because the idea strikes him as grossly unnatural. He realizes that he may be increasing the danger of contacting tularemia or other parasites, but he also examines the organs of any animal he kills and he never kills for food any animal that appears sick or lethargic. Illness usually shows rapidly and dramatically in small animals. It is always best to clean your hands with disinfectant after processing small game, especially rabbits.

FIELD DRESSING SMALL GAME

All small animals should be bled, skinned, and cleaned as soon after the kill as possible. The animal should not be transported any distance until it is properly cleaned. Once cleaned, the carcass may be wrapped in leaves or grass and safely carried in a shoulder pack or game pouch.

Bleeding is a good precaution in all cases and is essential in many. The idea is to drain the carcass of as much blood as possible so that it will not stiffen in the tissues of the meat and make the meat tough and strong tasting. Often, bleeding is not necessary if the animal was hit by a high velocity bullet or if the fatal wound was in the neck, lungs, or heart. However, experience is the only adequate teacher of when and when not to bleed, so it's best to make it a practice. Parp bleeds every animal he kills.

The most common method of bleeding an animal is simply to cut its throat all the way across. Another method is to cut from the breastbone up to the windpipe. This is an effective way to cut major arteries and veins. Before using either method, hang the animal upside down or hold it by its rear legs.

Skinning is the next step. You should always skin soon after the kill; this allows the carcass to cool much more rapidly than it would with the skin on. Small animals are also much easier to skin before you gut them than afterward. Usually small game is skinned by the quickest and easiest method possible. People rarely try to

save the skins of small animals because they are very difficult to handle and cure. There are exceptions.

Parp's skinning method for most small animals is quite simple. With a small sharp scissors, he makes a slit in the skin at the center of the back, cutting through the skin only, not the thin layer of meat or fat underneath. With the point of the scissors, he holds the skin away from the muscle or membrane underneath and cuts all around the body, separating the skin into two sections. He is careful not to puncture the membrane over the stomach and intestines. Inserting two fingers from each hand under the skin, he pulls both the sections of skin away. He then slips the top skin up the neck to the head and up the fore legs as far as possible. It will turn inside out. The bottom half of the skin will stop at the joints of the rear legs and the tail. He then simply uses scissors to cut wherever necessary. He cuts the legs off close to the joints where the skin stopped slipping. Then he cuts off the head and the animal is skinned.

To eviscerate the animal, it is necessary to use the point of a small, very sharp knife to slit from the breastbone down to and around the vent. Insert your fingers at the top of the cut and get hold of the windpipe. Pull down, thus removing all the innards at once. Locate the heart and liver and save them, unless you want to eat them on the spot as some hunters do. They are most nutritious.

Before you eat anything, however, you should examine the heart, lungs, and liver of the animal. If you see signs of discoloration, white spots, or parasites, burn the carcass and the skin and forget about it. In 30 years of hunting, Parp can count on one hand the number of diseased animals he's killed.

Some larger, small-game animals will require a somewhat different procedure. If you are interested in saving the hide of a muskrat, groundhog, marmot, or beaver, Parp suggests you consult an expert or study one of the many fine books on the subject. There are special skinning techniques, especially when dealing with potentially fine furs like beaver. In any case, it's best to gut these larger animals before skinning. When you do so, avoid leaving hairs on the meat.

HANGING AND BUTCHERING SMALL GAME

Hanging is the process of suspending a skinned and cleaned carcass in an open area of circulating air in the neighborhood of 38°F. Hanging improves the flavor and texture of red meat because enzymes act to break down some of the fibers of the meat. Rabbits and larger animals are best hung for four or five days. Squirrels and smaller animals should be prepared without hanging, or hung for one or two days only.

To hang small game, simply suspend it by one leg from a hook, or string it from a nail. Be sure no scavengers can reach the meat, and be careful to protect the area from sunlight, precipitation, and insects. Frequently alternate the hanging leg on rabbits and larger animals.

Many people simply freeze wild meat without hanging it and there are circumstances that make this desirable: for example, you might kill a nice woodchuck in July and not have an area cool enough to hang the animal safely. Freezing does tenderize meat, though much more slowly and less satisfactorily than hanging. If you freeze game without hanging it, be sure it's well bled and then freeze it as soon as the body heat is gone.

If you take your small game home and cook it before it stiffens, the meat will be tender even without hanging.

BAKED SQUIRREL WITH WILD RICE STUFFING

This recipe is for the best, most tender, and meaty squirrels. Parp says it's most suitable for fat gray squirrels.

2 or 3	plump squirrels, cleaned and skinned
1	quart Wild Herb Vinegar (page 68)
2	tablespoons lemon juice
1	teaspoon cayenne pepper
2	tablespoons corn oil
1	medium wild onion, chopped
4	cups Wild Rice Stuffing (page 108)

Preheat oven to 350°F.

Soak squirrels overnight in the vinegar.

Remove squirrels from vinegar and wipe dry with paper towels. Cut into meaty serving portions. Season with lemon juice and cayenne pepper.

Heat corn oil in a heavy skillet, but do not allow to smoke. Sauté onion in hot oil until translucent.

Brown squirrel lightly in oil with onions. Don't try for a dark brown; squirrel dries easily. Remove from heat.

Arrange squirrel on a bed of Wild Rice Stuffing in a heavy, covered casserole dish. Cover with onions.

Bake, covered, for 45 minutes.

Remove cover and bake an additional 15 minutes.

Yield: *2 – 4 servings*

SQUIRREL PIE

2 squirrels, cut in 3 pieces each

3 cups stock, boiling

3 tablespoons wild rice flour

1 teaspoon coltsfoot ash

⅛ teaspoon cayenne pepper

½ cup wild mushroom pieces

½ cup wild celery stalks, chopped

1 prepared pie crust

milk

Cover squirrel pieces with stock and simmer 1 hour.

Preheat oven to 350°F.

Remove bones from cooked meat.

Add flour, coltsfoot ash, cayenne, mushrooms, and celery to stock.

Return meat to pot and mix in thoroughly.

Place mixture in deep baking dish.

Roll and shape pie crust to fit over filling in baking dish. Slit crust for steam to escape and brush with milk.

Bake until crust is golden brown, about 40 minutes. To serve, break crust into pieces and cover with filling.

Yield: *6 servings*

SQUIRREL STEW
WITH PARP'S DUMPLINGS

Here's how to use those scrawny squirrels that aren't quite good enough for baking. Since only skinny squirrels grow in the San Juan Mountains, Parp has had many opportunities to test this recipe. Naturally, good fat squirrels make an even better stew.

4 or 5	small squirrels
2	tablespoons corn oil
2½	cups lima beans, soaked overnight and then cooked
2	cups nut grass kernels (*or* corn)
1	teaspoon freshly ground tarragon
1	wild onion, chopped
2	cups Indian potatoes, cut in pieces
6	wild carrots, cut in pieces
4	cups stewed tomatoes (*or* ground cherries)
2	tablespoons honey

arrowroot (*or* cornstarch) (optional)

Parp's Dumplings (page 308)

Cut squirrels into small serving pieces. If they are large and meaty, remove the meat from the bones.

Heat oil in a skillet. Lightly brown squirrel meat.

Place browned squirrel and cooked lima beans in a stew pot or Crock-Pot. Add nut grass kernels, tarragon, onion, potatoes, and carrots. Cover with water that you've allowed to cool slightly after boiling.

Simmer for at least 2½ hours. Add tomatoes and honey. Simmer at least 30 minutes longer. If necessary, thicken with arrowroot or cornstarch.

Prepare Parp's Dumplings. Drop by spoonfuls into the stew. Simmer uncovered until the dumplings are cooked, about 15 minutes, then serve with salad.

Yield: *6 servings*

FRIED SQUIRREL

½	teaspoon coltsfoot ash
¼	teaspoon cayenne pepper
½	cup cornmeal (*or acorn meal*)
2 or 3	squirrels
1	egg, beaten
3	tablespoons corn oil
1	wild onion, sliced
1	teaspoon lemon juice

Combine coltsfoot, cayenne, and cornmeal in a bag.

Cut squirrel into serving pieces and dip in beaten egg.

Heat corn oil in a large, heavy skillet. Do not allow oil to smoke. Sauté onion slices, then remove.

Shake squirrel pieces with cornmeal. Brown in oil.

Reduce heat to low and replace onion. Sprinkle with lemon juice. Cover and simmer 45 minutes.

Remove cover for 10 minutes. Serve immediately.

Yield: *2–4 servings*

RABBIT STEW

- 1 rabbit
- 3 cups stock, boiling
- 2 tablespoons peanut oil
- 2 cups Indian potatoes, cut in pieces
- ½ cup wild celery stalks, chopped
- 4 wild carrots, cut in pieces
- 2 wild onions, sliced
- 1 cup stewed tomatoes (*or* Ground Cherry Sauce [page 102])
- 1 tablespoon fresh chives, chopped
- ½ teaspoon tarragon
- ¼ cup wild rice flour

Place whole rabbit in hot stock to cover and simmer 2 hours. Drain and reserve stock.

Allow rabbit to cool. Remove bones and cut meat into chunks.

Heat peanut oil in a large pot. Add Indian potatoes, wild celery, carrots, and onions. Cover and cook 20 minutes.

Add tomatoes and stock to vegetables. Increase heat. Simmer 5 minutes.

Add rabbit meat, chives, and tarragon. Simmer 20 minutes before thickening with flour.

Yield: *4 servings*

BAKED STUFFED RABBIT

This recipe of Parp's has evolved through many cotton-tails. The secret is in the rye bread stuffing.

    1 cup stock

    3 cups dry rye bread crumbs

    1 teaspoon coltsfoot ash

    ½ teaspoon peppergrass seeds

    ⅛ teaspoon thyme

    ⅛ teaspoon sage

    ⅛ teaspoon rosemary

    ⅛ teaspoon nutmeg

    1 cup wild celery stalks, chopped

    2 rabbits

    6 wild carrots, cut in pieces

Preheat oven to 350°F.

Warm ½ cup of the stock in a pot. Add bread crumbs and toss to moisten bread evenly. Add seasonings.

Add celery to bread. Stuff rabbits and skewer closed.

Place stuffed rabbits in a baking pan with wild carrots alongside. Cover with a cooking cloth and soak this with ½ of the remaining stock.

Bake for 20 minutes. Add remaining stock. Bake and baste frequently another 40 minutes.

Remove cooking cloth. Bake 15 minutes and serve.

Yield: *4 – 6 servings*

HASENPFEFFER

This traditional German recipe is a delicious way to prepare older rabbits. It predates the refrigerator by centuries, and the marinade is a method of preserving the meat as well as cleansing, tenderizing, seasoning, and preparing it. Parp has often kept unrefrigerated rabbit in the marinade for weeks at a time. The longer the marinating time, the better the Hasenpfeffer.

Marinade

- 3 wild onions, sliced
- 2 cups Wild Herb Vinegar (page 68)
- 1 clove garlic, minced
- 8 whole peppercorns
- ½ teaspoon tarragon
- 4 whole fresh cloves
- 1 bay leaf
- 4 wild carrots, chopped
- ¼ teaspoon basil
- 1 teaspoon coltsfoot ash

Other Ingredients

- 2 rabbits, cut in serving pieces
- 1 teaspoon coltsfoot ash
- 1 teaspoon peppergrass seeds
- ¼ cup corn oil

2 **wild onions, finely chopped**

1 **cup rye bread crumbs, dried**

¾ **cup yogurt**

Begin at least 2 − 3 days before the intended meal. In a large earthenware casserole, mix together all marinade ingredients. Let stand at room temperature for 1 hour.

Add rabbit so that all pieces are well coated with marinade. If necessary, add additional vinegar to barely cover. Cover casserole tightly and place in a cool, dark place (unrefrigerated) for at least 48 hours. Turn rabbit pieces every 6 hours or so.

After marinating time is over, remove rabbit pieces and dry with a clean cloth. Rub well with coltsfoot ash and peppergrass seeds.

Heat corn oil in a large skillet and brown rabbit pieces. When browned, add onions. Add 1 cup of the marinade liquid and bring to a slow simmer. Cover and simmer until marimade is nearly gone, about 4 hours. Add an additional ¾ cup marinade and cook an additional 20 minutes.

Remove rabbit pieces and keep warm. Add crisp bread crumbs and yogurt to hot marinade in skillet. Cook slowly and stir until mixture thickens.

Place rabbit pieces in a heated serving dish. Cover with yogurt/marinade sauce. Stir and serve.

Yield: *4 − 6 servings*

PORCUPINE STEW

Folklore to the contrary, porcupines are exceedingly clean and desirable meat animals. Unlike opossums, they are strict vegetarians and the only thing that will draw them away from fresh greens is salt. When they chew axe handles, rifle stocks, porch rails, and the like, they aren't after rotting wood or insects, as many suppose. They're after the salt residue of human perspiration. Porcupines are not scavengers and will starve before eating meat, fresh or otherwise. Parp has not killed a porcupine in many years, because of a personal superstition, but he is always glad to help a friend dispose of any excess porcupine meat, especially livers. It is now illegal to hunt porcupines in most areas, but in case you ever find one in the far North woods, here's an easy and delicious stew.

1	fresh porcupine, whole
1½	teaspoons tarragon
1	cup wild rice
3	potatoes, cut in pieces
3	carrots, cut in pieces
1	cup raisins (*or* currants)
1	teaspoons honey
¼	cup cornstarch

Clean and skin the porcupine carefully, starting with the belly. (To remove quills from the flesh, use a scissors to snip the quill in the center. This releases the barb and allows the quill to be pulled straight out.)

Place the skinned carcass in a large pot. Cover with water that has cooled slightly from boiling.

Bring water to a simmer and cook for 20 minutes.

Remove porcupine from water and allow to cool slightly. Cut meat away from bones in chunks. Place pieces in fresh hot water and simmer an additional 20 minutes.

Add tarragon, rice, potatoes, carrots, raisins, and honey. Simmer together for 1 hour.

Add cornstarch, stir, and cook until thickened. Serve immediately.

Yield: *4 — 6 servings*

DEEP COAL-BAKED PORCUPINE IN THE HIDE

Here's a recipe for the adventurous. Parp first enjoyed this porcupine recipe while roaming the northern Michigan woods with a Huron Indian friend. Here's how the Natives used to do it.

Disembowel one fresh porcupine but leave the skin and quills intact. Dig a hole in sandy soil about 2 feet deep by 2 feet in diameter. Start a good hardwood fire in the hole and allow the fire to burn down to hot glowing coals. Scrape the coals to form a cavity with coals evenly spread around the sides and bottoms of the hole.

Place your porcupine in the hole, quills down on the coals. Cover the body cavity with a lid or piece of cloth to keep it clean. Then completely cover the porcupine and the hole with earth. Go fishing or take a nap. In 2 or 3 hours, unearth 1 cooked porcupine. The coals remove the quills and outer skin and bake the meat thoroughly. Season with finely crushed wood ashes. Eat by opening the body cavity and digging your knife into the succulent portions of the meat.

PORCUPINE LIVER

Porcupine liver is undeniably one of the tastiest and most nutritious edibles that you could ever drag out of the woods. It is widely considered a delicacy by woods people all over North America—those are folks who like to disagree with each other just for the fun of it.

Parp remembers once, as a boy, sitting with his older cousin in the forests of southern Illinois waiting and watching for a wandering porcupine. After so much time passed that he forgot what he was watching for, Parp heard a faint rustle of leaves and sticks. Suddenly, in the gathering dusk, a porcupine appeared, snuffling and snorting, its curious and finely intelligent face turned precisely in their direction. One shot from the older boy's gun and the best of days was over, both for the hunters and the porcupine. After a few hours' work, the skinned and cleaned carcass was soaking in an ancient pot while the liver simmered gently on the cookstove, ample reward for the hunters' patience.

Here is an alternative to the traditional recipe, which calls for bacon fat, salt, pepper, and flour. Any small-game liver may be prepared in the same manner.

- 1 porcupine liver
- ½ cup rye flour
- ¼ teaspoon sage
- ⅛ teaspoon rosemary
- ⅛ teaspoon thyme
- ¼ cup corn oil
- ½ teaspoon Wild Herb Vinegar (page 68)

1 teaspoon lemon juice

1 teaspoon watercress, chopped

Clean liver and slice about ¼ inch thick. Combine flour and herbs. Dredge liver slices in this mixture.

Heat corn oil in a heavy skillet. When hot, add Wild Herb Vinegar. This will sputter considerably.

Lightly sauté liver slices in hot oil over moderate heat. Do not overcook. Turn once only, when underside is lightly browned.

When both sides are browned, sprinkle with lemon juice and watercress. Serve immediately.

Yield: *2 servings*

porcupine

Woodchucks and Marmots

Woodchucks (or groundhogs) are plentiful throughout most of North America, especially in farmlands. Like porcupines, they are strict vegetarians and will eat only fresh green vegetation, wild or domestic. The only requirements for sweet, flavorful groundhog meat are proper cleaning, including the removal of the glands under the front legs, and proper hanging time. When you clean a groundhog, remove the front leg glands first and be sure to clean your knife before using it in the rest of the meat.

Marmots are the high-country version of the groundhog. The yellow-bellied marmot is the most common and is found throughout the Rocky Mountains. The hoary marmot is principally a resident of the Olympic Mountain Range in Washington.

Marmots are wonderful beings. They possess a tantalizing sense of humor and have been known to stand around in groups and make fun of cowboys who climb rocks in high-heeled, pointy-toed boots. They are also very musical creatures who will emerge from their cleverly concealed hiding places to attend a high-meadow harmonica concert, and may even join in with a whistling chorus. Devoted homebodies, they are friendly and loyal to their families. They are also capable of turning into rocks when pursued, bothered, or spied upon. They simply fold their legs and become solid, flat, gray rocks that whistle.

Most folks parboil chucks or marmots. The meat can be quite strong. It is a flavor that can grow on you, but few of us have the opportunity to eat marmots regularly. In any case, parboiling or marinating will most often improve the flavor and quality of the meat.

Woodchucks and marmots are best hung first by a hind leg, then by a front leg, alternating frequently. The length of hanging varies, of course, with temperature, humidity, and altitude. Correct hanging will result in highly flavorful and tender meat if the hanging is terminated just before tainting occurs.

Each year, nimrods in North America kill thousands of woodchucks. Since woodchucks are rodents and do not have a reputation as good table fare, the majority of the carcasses are discarded and left to rot into an unsanitary threat to everything living in the area.

Now, Parp would shoot an obnoxious critter such as a wharf rat or a Pomeranian, and would decline to feast on the remains. But groundhogs, marmots, porcupines, and others do not deserve their reputations as inedible. Properly treated, they can provide marvelous dinners. So, says Parp, they should never be viewed as targets for varmint shooters. They deserve the dignity of being properly cleaned, cooked, and devoured.

woodchuck

BAKED MARMOT OR WOODCHUCK DINNER

This recipe is good for large woodchucks but is best for fat, high-altitude, yellow-bellied marmots.

- 2 quarts water to cover
- ¼ cup Wild Herb Vinegar (page 68)
- 1 marmot or woodchuck
- 4 sweet potatoes (*or* wild caraway roots)
- 1 teaspoon peppergrass seeds
- ¼ teaspoon thyme
- 2 tablespoons lemon juice
- 4 wild apples, cored and stuffed with raisins and honey

Combine water and vinegar in a large pot. Bring to boil, then allow to cool slightly.

Place cleaned carcass in vinegar and simmer until tender, about 1½ hours. Preheat oven to 300°F. Meanwhile, boil potatoes until done, or steam caraway roots.

Remove tender carcass from water and dry with a cloth.

Place carcass in a baking dish and rub with peppergrass seeds and thyme. Sprinkle with lemon juice.

Surround meat with sweet potatoes and stuffed apples. Bake, basting often, for 1½ hours.

Serve with Steamed Wild Rice (page 298) and Parp's Wild Chutney (page 103).

Yield: *6 servings*

BRAISED WOODCHUCK

½ cup corn oil

1 teaspoon Wild Herb Vinegar (page 68)

½ cup rye flour

½ teaspoon coltsfoot ash

1 teaspoon cayenne pepper

1 or 2 woodchucks, cut in serving pieces

1 cup wild onions, chopped

1 clove garlic, chopped

1 cup Dark Game Stock (page 72)

1 bay leaf

Preheat oven to 325°F.

Place corn oil in a roasting pan and heat. When hot, add Wild Herb Vinegar.

Mix flour, coltsfoot ash, and cayenne in a sack. Add woodchuck pieces one at a time and shake to coat.

Brown coated woodchuck in hot oil. Remove browned pieces and sauté onion and garlic together. Add Wild Game Stock over medium heat. Bring to simmer. Return meat to pan and add bay leaf.

Cover and bake for 3 hours. Serve with baked carrots and cranberry sauce, or baked potatoes and salad.

Yield: *4 — 6 servings*

SAN JUAN MARMOT STEW

Parp must admit that he can't remember which member of the Creede Repertory Theatre group donated this recipe. Parp's debt is great, however, as this is the surest way to come up with a fine marmot dinner.

    1 whole marmot, cleaned

    1 gallon water at room temperature

    1 cup Wild Herb Vinegar (page 68)

    1 whole onion

hot water to cover

    4 tablespoons corn oil

    2 large yellow onions, sliced thin

    2 teaspoons tamari soy sauce

    6 wild carrots, cut and sliced

    1 tablespoon wild rice flour

   ½ teaspoon tarragon

   ⅛ teaspoon rosemary

   ⅛ teaspoon thyme

1½ cups stock

yogurt, to thicken sauce

Soak cleaned and skinned marmot overnight in combined water, vinegar, and onion.

Remove marmot from vinegar solution. Rinse. Place in water that has cooled slightly from boiling. Simmer for 1 hour, skimming surface frequently.

Remove from heat. Cool 1 hour in cooking water.

When cool, remove the marmot from the water and wipe with a damp cloth. Remove bones and cut meat into cubes.

Heat oven to 300°F.

Heat 1 tablespoon oil in heavy skillet. Brown ½ of the cubed marmot meat. Remove from pan. Add another tablespoon of oil and brown remaining meat. Do not overcook; cooking at this high temperature will toughen marmot meat.

Place browned meat in a large covered casserole.

Sauté onion until translucent. Cover marmot meat with sautéed onion. Pour tamari soy sauce on top. Place carrots around outside of casserole.

Mix together flour, tarragon, rosemary, and thyme. Sprinkle over meat.

Place in oven for 20 minutes. Remove and add stock by pouring around meat. Return to oven and bake for 3 hours.

Remove baked meat to a hot plate and keep warm. Remove any scum or fat from the surface of the casserole liquid. Beat in yogurt by tablespoons. Correct sauce seasoning.

Cover meat with sauce and serve immediately with baked potatoes, wild rice, or wild vegetables.

Yield: *6 servings*

ROAST STUFFED RACCOON

Raccoons are not vegetarians and in fact will eat almost anything. However, they are not usually scavengers and prefer to catch living creatures such as frogs, crayfish, and aquatic insects. They rarely raid chicken coops, a trespass of which they are often suspected, but they love to get into garbage.

Because of the raccoon's varied diet, its flesh is dark red and quite strong. It can be appetizing if properly prepared. Fresh raccoon meat should always be soaked in vinegar water before preparing. If the animal is to be frozen, it should be hung for 48 hours first. As with most strong meat, recipes for raccoon should be kept simple and spices or seasonings should be very light, or reserved until after cooking.

    1 raccoon

    1 quart boiling water

    ½ cup Wild Herb Vinegar (page 68)

    1 recipe Wild Onion Stuffing (page 110) *or* Wild Apple Dressing [page 109])

    6 wild onions, quartered

    1 cooking cloth, soaked with corn oil

    2 cups Dark Game Stock (page 72)

Remove all surface fat from the cleaned raccoon. Place in solution of water and Wild Herb Vinegar that has cooled slightly from boiling. Simmer for 1 hour while skimming surface frequently. Meanwhile, preheat oven to 375°F.

Drain raccoon, pat dry, and stuff. Place breast-down in a roasting pan with legs tucked under. Surround with quartered onions. Cover with oil-soaked cooking cloth. Add Wild Game Stock.

Place in oven for 15 minutes, then reduce heat to 325°F and roast 1 hour, basting frequently. Allow to cool slightly before serving.

Yield: *4 servings*

Muskrat

The muskrat (or musquash) is found all over the northern United States as well as Canada. It is one of the most useful animals and has supplied meat, fur, and tools for North Americans since prehistory.

Muskrat meat compares favorably to beef in both nutrition and flavor. It has less fat than beef, as much protein, fewer calories, and is higher in thiamin and riboflavin. When properly cleaned and prepared, muskrat is wonderfully delicious, dark, and rich.

Like many water dwellers and other small animals, the muskrat carries scent glands that must be carefully removed immediately after the kill. A muskrat has two of these glands, located on either side of the base of the tail. Remove them with a very sharp and pointed knife with a small blade. Be sure not to use the same knife in the meat afterwards unless you clean it thoroughly with hot water and soap.

In addition to its nutritional and fur value, the muskrat is a desirable resident of our streams, ponds, and marshes. In many areas, though, its delicate environment is threatened by chemicals and other pollutants.

MUSKRAT STEW

- 2 muskrats
- 1 gallon water at room temperature
- 1 apple, quartered
- 1 cup plus 1 tablespoon Wild Herb Vinegar (page 68)
- ¼ cup corn oil
- 3 wild onions, sliced
- 1½ cups Wild Vegetable Stock (page 77)
- 1 bay leaf
- ⅓ cup nut grass tubers
- ⅛ teaspoon sage
- ⅛ teaspoon rosemary
- ⅛ teaspoon thyme
- 2 tablespoons rye flour
- ½ cup cold water
- ¾ cup yogurt
- 1 teaspoon fresh chives, chopped

Clean muskrats. Combine water, apple, and 1 cup Wild Herb Vinegar. Add muskrats and soak overnight.

Drain muskrats, pat dry, and cut into serving pieces. Heat oil in a stew pot and lightly brown muskrat pieces. Remove and sauté onion slices. Replace muskrat.

Add stock, bay leaf, tubers, herbs, and 1 tablespoon Wild Herb Vinegar. Bring to point of boiling, reduce heat and simmer, covered, 1 hour. Remove meat.

Combine flour and water. Stir into pot liquid and stir while cooking for 5 minutes. Stir in yogurt and chives.

Serve with Steamed Wild Rice (page 298).

Yield: *4 servings*

ROAST MUSKRAT

- 1 gallon water at room temperature
- 1¼ cup Wild Herb Vinegar (page 68)
- 2 muskrats
- ½ teaspoon peppergrass seeds
- ½ teaspoon coltsfoot ash
- ½ cup safflower oil
- ⅓ cup acorn meal
- 4 cups Wild Rice Stuffing (page 108)

Combine water and 1 cup Wild Herb Vinegar. Soak cleaned muskrats overnight.

Preheat oven to 325°F.

Drain muskrats and pat dry. Combine peppergrass seeds, coltsfoot ash, safflower oil, and acorn meal.

Stuff muskrats with Wild Rice Stuffing. Place on rack in a roasting pan. Spread mixture on muskrats.

Roast uncovered, until browned, then add ¼ cup Wild Herb Vinegar and cover tightly. Continue roasting an additional 45 minutes. Serve immediately.

Yield: *6 servings*

BEAVER ROAST

When cleaning beaver, remember to remove the scent glands from under the front legs and along the spine near the small of the back. It's always best to cook beaver slowly and with plenty of liquid. The meat should sit overnight in a mixture of cold water to cover and 1 cup Wild Herb Vinegar. Before cooking, rinse the meat in cool water and pat dry.

- 1 beaver, cleaned and prepared
- 2 cloves garlic, minced
- ½ teaspoon paprika
- 4 cups Wild Rice Stuffing (page 108)
- 1 cooking cloth, soaked with corn oil
- 4 carrots, cut and sliced (*or* potatoes *or* wild tubers)
- ½ cup water

Preheat oven to 325°F.

Rub cleaned beaver with garlic.

Sprinkle with paprika.

Stuff and place belly-down in a large roasting pan. Cover with cooking cloth.

Surround beaver with carrots. Add the water.

Roast, covered, for 3 hours. Check frequently and add more water, ¼ cup at a time, to maintain moisture.

Yield: *4 servings*

CROCK-POT BEAVER

This beaver recipe from Parp's old friend, Three-Legged Muskrat, is one of Parp's all-time favorites. It is certainly the easiest, most foolproof beaver recipe of all.

    1 beaver (*or* 2 beaver tails, skinned)
    1 tablespoon lemon juice
    1 bay leaf
    ¼ teaspoon paprika
    ⅛ teaspoon rosemary
    ⅛ teaspoon thyme
    2 wild onions, chopped
    4 wild carrots, cut in pieces
    1 cup Indian potatoes, cut in pieces (*or* other wild *or* domestic vegetables)

Place beaver in Crock-Pot or Dutch oven. Add water to cover.

Add lemon juice, bay leaf, paprika, herbs, and onions. Cover and simmer slowly for 8 to 24 hours.

Two hours before serving, add carrots and Indian potatoes. Correct seasoning.

Serve spooned over Steamed Wild Rice (page 298)

Yield: *4 servings*

CHAPTER TEN

NORTH AMERICAN BIG GAME

In the meadows, huge creatures of ultimate mystery reflect on memories of another age or murmur gently of the wonders of watercress and gushing springs. Grass and water, forests and mountains. A perfect male brushes lovingly against a perfect female as their offspring sprint and tumble under the enormous sun.

If we are what we eat, do elk hunters put on the grace, dignity, and awareness of these pure and magnificent beings? Perhaps. Many hunters genuinely love the wilderness and shun the drunken carnage of hunting season. They walk, rather than ride. Only by walking can a hunter know the environment of the hunted. And that, we believe, is essential.

FIELD DRESSING BIG GAME

Immediately after the kill, a large animal should be bled, eviscerated, and skinned. This allows the meat to cool quickly and removes parts that may contaminate it.

Cleaning and skinning a large animal is not a complex operation, but it is hard work. If you can arrange to kill your animal in the late afternoon you'll be better off. Ideally there will be enough light for the job (perhaps two hours or more), and the carcass can hang in the cool air all night rather than dry out under a hot sun.

The best tools for the job are two or three sharp pointed knives, a broad-swept skinning knife, a good stone and steel for sharpening and honing, a small meat saw, and a length of rope or light block and tackle; some people carry one knife only and manage to get the job done. If you start the job close to dusk, you ought to have at least two dependable flashlights on hand. Parp uses a small backpacking light and holds it in his teeth to leave both hands free.

Start by cutting the animal's throat all the way across and clear back to the neck bone. If the animal is on the ground, try to arrange it so that the head is lower than the tail. If you're suspending the animal for cleaning, hang it head down. Immediately cut the throat and bleed thoroughly.

Suspend the animal, if possible, from a tree limb, using a light block and tackle. If you must dress the animal on the ground, use a length of rope to tie the body open by one hind leg, or have a companion hold one leg under tension.

To open the body, start with a small, sharp knife of pointed shape. It will quickly dull, so keep a stone or steel within reach. You should also have a length of string for tying off the intestines.

Many people shudder at the idea of gutting an animal, especially a large animal, feeling that it is a disgusting process. It isn't, or needn't be. If done properly, all of the internal organs, including stomach and intestines, come out together in one package with a minimum of mess.

Insert the point of your first knife at the top of the breastbone. Slit the skin to the bottom of the breastbone. Then use the fingers of your other hand to lift the hide. This will allow you to slit the skin over the abdominal cavity without cutting the stomach or intestines. Slide your hand along behind your knife to lift away the hide as you slit it from the breastbone to the genitals. When you reach the genitals, cut around them to free them from the carcass. Then cut out the rectum. Slip your hand down close to the hip bone on one side and grasp the large intestine. With just a little more knife work, you can probably now pull the intestine free. Use a piece of string to tie it near the end.

Return to the upper part of the body. With a fresh knife, slit the skin from the breastbone up to the throat. The skin should now be open all the way from the throat to the crotch. Use a pointed game saw or heavy knife or ax to split the breastbone. Cut as necessary to free the

windpipe and gullet. Grasp the windpipe in one hand and pull downward. As you pull, all of the internal organs will lift up, out of the body cavity. Use a sharp knife to cut as necessary. Pull the windpipe back and cut until all of the entrails are completely removed from throat to crotch. Be very careful not to cut the stomach, intestines, or genitals. Also take care to keep hair from contaminating the meat.

Once the animal is eviscerated you may notice a large pool of blood lying in the chest cavity, if you're working on the ground. Use a clean cloth to soak up this blood. Force the rib cage open and use a stick to keep it that way. This will speed the cooling process. Do not use water on the meat at any time. Hair can be washed off the meat with vinegar either in the field or at home. Many people prefer to cut away all bloodshot meat as they encounter it, but Parp likes to wait until the animal is hanging in the meat room at home.

The heart, tongue, liver, kidneys, and brains of all large animals are delicious edibles. Once the animal is field dressed, remove these parts from the rest of the viscera. Store them in the chest cavity if your animal is to cool on the ground all night, or grill one or more of these organs for a proud feast on the first night.

To remove the tongue, place the head facedown on the ground. Cut along the inside of the jaw until you can lift up the tongue. Cut it off at the base, along with any fat you find there. Wash the tongue in vinegar, if available, and scrape it well.

To remove the brains, simply split the skull with an ax

or saw. Use a small knife to make any necessary cuts, and lift the brains out with both hands. Wash off any blood with vinegar.

Circumstances will determine whether you skin the animal in the field or at home. It's best, when possible, to remove the hide at once. This allows the carcass to cool much faster. In some areas, the law requires you to leave the skin on until you reach home. Also, if you must move your animal some distance before you butcher it, the hide will help to keep dirt away from the meat. In any case, you should always remove the hide before quartering. Otherwise, the hide is wasted—a terrible crime—and hair will contaminate the best portions of the meat.

If you're going to leave your animal in the field overnight, the best procedure is to remove the hide from all areas except the back. This way the carcass cools quickly and the back of the animal, resting on the ground, is protected from dirt. Cover the animal with snow or spruce boughs.

SKINNING A LARGE ANIMAL

Patience. That's what it takes. Practice helps, but only patient care will result in a clean, uncut hide of proper pattern, detail, and thickness. Many old hands will ruin a hide, despite their experience, if they are rushed by cold or other circumstances.

Use a swept-blade skinning knife, a specialized tool designed to strip the hide away from the carcass without puncturing or cutting the skin. Your objective is to

remove the hide completely and cleanly. There should be no meat on the hide when removed, and no hide on the meat. Again, patience is called for.

Start at the neck with the head removed. Use one hand to pull the skin away from the carcass. Pull the knife in sweeping motions with the edge in the direction of the hide. Proceeding in this fashion, with the animal on its back, skin the neck down to the shoulder.

Cut the skin of each leg from the body cavity to the first joint. Cut the skin around each leg at this point. Now, using your knife as little as possible, pull the hide away from the legs and down along the sides. Some parts of the hide will strip away quite easily. If the animal is hanging, you should be able to pull the whole hide down and off.

If you have never skinned a large animal before, you may not recognize that the fibrous material between the hide and the meat is fat. The fat should stay with the carcass.

When the hide is removed, rub it thoroughly with plenty of coarse salt. Thus salted, a clean hide will keep until you get around to tanning it.

CARE OF BIG-GAME MEAT

Once your animal is dressed and skinned, the problems of transporting the carcass will determine your next step, as will the legal requirements of your state. Since Parp carries the meat out on foot, he usually proceeds with quartering and boning out most of the meat. If he doesn't have far to go, he may simply quarter the animal and pack out the quarters. This is best as it is most convenient to hang the meat in quarters and cut it up for freezing after the aging is complete.

If you must leave some of your meat in the field, be sure to protect it from birds and insects. The human smell will discourage most other scavengers, such as coyotes, for at least one week. Bright rags tied to nearby branches will keep the birds away. The best protection from insects is a thick coat of ground black pepper rubbed into the meat. The pepper also helps to cure the meat and contributes to a firm rind.

We have found it best, when several trips are necessary, to pack out the hide, heart, liver, kidneys, and brains on the first trip. This gets the most perishable items home first and leaves the meat to begin aging naturally in the open air. We leave the quarters as exposed as possible, but covered with spruce boughs or hung high in a tree, out of reach. You can then come back with help, in a week or so, and pack out the quarters or the boned meat. All of this assumes that the season is autumn and that daytime temperatures don't exceed 40°F, or so.

The meat of either elk or deer should be hung in fresh circulating air at about 38°F for at least ten days, or as much as four weeks. This process is essential if you plan to eat any of the meat fairly soon. If you plan to freeze the meat and keep it for six months before eating, you may choose to skip the hanging. Freezing will tenderize and age meat in exactly the same way as hanging. It just takes a lot longer.

NORTH
AMERICAN
BIG
GAME

CUTTING AND WRAPPING

After hanging in quarters for about ten days, meat is ready to process for the freezer. You want to waste as little as possible and you want the packages you freeze to be convenient for cooking when you're ready for them. The size of your family, the extent to which you use red meat in your meals, and the type of animal you're processing will determine the exact cuts you make and their size. Remember, though, that while small packages freeze more easily, large cuts keep better with less chance of drying.

If you've used pepper to protect your meat in the field and in hanging, you should remove the pepper with the rind before freezing the meat. Pepper may cause the meat to age more than you'd wish, even while frozen.

The drawing here illustrates the most common cuts of meat made from big-game animals. especially venison. Elk cuts are closer to this illustration than are deer cuts. A deer is much smaller than an elk and may not contain enough meat to make all of these cuts. You will soon develop your own system for cutting meats to fit your needs. The process is described here in general terms.

First, remove all hair, dirt, bloodshot meat, and rind. If necessary, wash the carcass with vinegar and clean sponges. Do not use water. Wipe away any blood that may spill.

If your deer or elk carcass is whole, start by splitting it

down the center of the back with a meat saw. Then divide each half into quarters by cutting upwards just below the last rib.

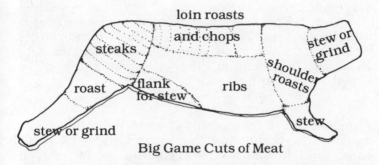

Big Game Cuts of Meat

Place one of the forequarters on a cutting table, inside down. Separate the plate from the ribs by scoring with a knife and then sawing through the bones. Remove the foreshank at the elbow and discard. Now remove the chuck by cutting between the fifth and sixth ribs. Saw through at the backbone. Bone out the neck and foreshanks. Divide the ribs into roasts or chops according to your needs.

To butcher the hindquarter, first remove any flank meat. Then separate the loin from the rump at the hip joint. The loin may either be boned and rolled, cut into several roasts, bone in, or cut into steaks. Elk loin steaks are unbeatable. Cut the rump into one or more boneless roasts, depending on the size of the animal. Then cut the round into half-round steaks. Bone out the upper rear shank meat for grinding. Cut all bones into pieces for stock and soups.

As the meat is cut, trimmed, and sized, you or a helper should immediately double-wrap each piece in good quality freezer paper. Your labeling should include the type of animal, the cut, approximate servings, the date of the kill, and the freezing date. If you wrap more than one piece in a package, place two sheets of waxed paper between each cut. This makes it easy to separate pieces for thawing. If you freeze your neck and shank meat in chunks to be ground or otherwise processed later, be sure to indicate this on your labels.

You should limit the amount of meat that you freeze at one time. If you attempt to freeze an entire elk all at once, you may lose both the elk and the freezer. We prefer to cut, wrap, and freeze one quarter at a time. The remainder benefits from longer aging.

Place your wrapped packages along the bottom and sides of your freezer. Do not put all of the packages together in a box and then set the box in the freezer. Later, after the meat is solidly frozen, you can reorganize it into small boxes.

Inspect your frozen packages regularly, perhaps once a month. If a wrapping becomes damaged or insecure, remove that cut. If it shows signs of drying, or freezer burn, cut away the damaged meat and use the good portion at once. Venison is very lean and is not contaminated by steroids, preservatives, or vitamins. Because of its purity, properly prepared and protected venison will far outlast commercial beef.

And what a gift it is.

VENISON TIPS

A sudden hush close in the woods. Far away, a high wind speaks of life continuing. Through brown leaves, a buff shade that doesn't move and almost blends. No matter how often you've been here before, you hear your heart, and nothing else. A line, drawn between you and the shape, a zap of Zeus's thunder, and the birds begin again; a rabbit pounds toward home.

So you have your venison. Whether it's wapiti or whitetail, moose or muley, it is venison. In the original Latin, the term venison applied to any quarry of the hunt. Now it refers to any deer or member of the deer family or a similar creature. Specifically, it refers to the meat of such an animal.

Moose meat is much more tender and marbled than the meat of deer or elk. For that reason, the cook need not be so concerned about drying the meat. Elk and deer are quite delicate and require special care to prevent drying. Overcooking is by far the greatest danger and is, unfortunately, widely practiced. People get the notion that the meat has to be purified by fire. Many cooks and others have written that venison should always be cooked thoroughly to be safe.

Bah. Cook any elk or deer meat approximately one-half as long as you would a similar cut of beef. Eat it very rare, extremely rare even, and do not attempt to char or crisp the meat.

Adding salt to uncooked venison is another common error. Salt dehydrates the meat almost immediately,

causes blood to interfere with the cooking, and greatly toughens the meat. It's hardly possible to make a worse mistake.

Venison should never be cooked while frozen. Like nearly every other meat, venison cooks best if allowed to reach room temperature first, ideally around 70°F. (We hope, for your sake and the meat's, that your rooms are warmer than ours.)

Nearly all of the recipes in this chapter work well with any wild meat. The venison recipes apply to elk, deer, moose, or caribou. Other recipes may call for a specific meat if considerations of the size, moisture, or peculiar taste of that meat apply.

Because venison can be overcooked so easily, Parp avoids ever mixing it with any other meat. No matter what you read elsewhere, it is not necessary or advisable to combine elk with beef when making elkburger. Pure venison, drained and ground fresh before freezing, will supply delicious, easy to broil burgers. Just don't broil them nearly as long as you would beef. If you have trouble with crumbling burgers, you are overcooking them. If you do not want to eat them rare, you may wish to mix in one beaten egg per pound of burger immediately before broiling. And broil them under the flame, not above.

Sausage is, of course, an exception and a compromise. People grind venison with pork shoulder meat and spices to produce sausage.

Many people mix their venison and pork in equal proportions. It's better to use more pork. Whatever amount of venison you use, you will have to overcook it in order to cook the pork thoroughly. Venison is probably best used in sausage as an extender, rather than as the main ingredient.

As we said before, we prefer slow, moist heat for all meat, especially wild game. It is easier to overcook meat if you're using a high, direct heat with no moisture added. If you use slow, moist heat you really have to work at overdoing it. Also, of course, slow cooking with moist heat is most likely to produce tender, evenly cooked meats for delicious and healthful wild meals.

BROILED ELK STEAKS

Elk steaks should be very lightly browned on both sides and heated almost all the way through. If they are cooked any longer, they are likely to toughen and will certainly lose much of their incomparable flavor. Although they make for a superb dinner, it's almost a shame to waste the energy they supply. One very rare elk steak for breakfast is good for a whole day of strenuous outdoor activity.

- 1 elk steak per person, about 2 inches thick
- 1 clove garlic, cut
- ¼ teaspoon fresh black pepper per steak

Preheat broiler.

Trim or clean each steak as necessary. Rub lightly with garlic and sprinkle with black pepper.

Place on rack under hot broiler. Brown each side lightly. Do not overcook.

ROAST ELK

This recipe calls for a large cut of elk, either the rump, loin, or saddle. A deer roast requires less heat for less time. A cut of moose requires less oil, less heat, and an adjustment in time determined by the size and cut.

We often prepare an elk roast dinner with steamed sweet potatoes and a salad for special visitors from civilization. Nearly everyone expresses surprise that elk really is so much more delicious than beef.

>   1 6- to 10-pound cut of elk
>   1 clove garlic
>   ½ cup corn oil
>   1 teaspoon peppergrass seeds
>   1 cooking cloth, soaked with corn oil
>   1 tablespoon hot water

Preheat oven to 500°F.

You may wish to rinse your roast with vinegar. Be sure to allow it to reach room temperature, or 70°F.

Rub the roast well with pieces of the garlic. Brush lightly with about ½ of the corn oil. Sprinkle with peppergrass seeds.

Place the roast on a rack in a large, uncovered roasting pan. Place in the oven for 5 minutes.

After 5 minutes, reduce the oven heat to 325°F. Roast as is for 25 more minutes.

Cover the roast with a cooking cloth saturated with corn oil. Return to oven and roast for at most 10 minutes to the pound. Ten minutes to the pound will produce a rare roast, but it's best even rarer. Baste as necessary to prevent drying. Use additional corn oil as needed. Halfway through, add the hot water to the bottom of the pan.

Remove the cooking cloth shortly before removing the roast from the oven.

Allow the roast to stand on a warm platter for 5 minutes, then serve with steamed wild vegetables and a wild salad.

Yield: *6 − 8 servings*

VICE GRIP ELK DINNER A LA THREE-LEGGED MUSKRAT

The Vice Grip Elk Dinner a la Muskrat is an annual event attended by Barnacle Parp's friends in the San Juan Mountains. On the appointed day, all the strange beings of this clan arise and go to a certain hot spring, in a certain mountain range, far away.

We take with us all that we need for our feast, including firewood, so as not to disturb the delicate balance of the sacred place. Some even take along a compatible lamb or goat for company. We stow all our gear and supplies

NORTH AMERICAN BIG GAME

between the huge easy chairs placed in the backs of the trucks. Passengers sit back in the easy chairs and munch wild nuts, berries, and mushrooms in the open air. Parp's friend Muskrat is always smart enough to drive, and arrives with a sharp appetite.

Finally, we arrive and gladly leave the vehicles behind. After a good hike to the spring, most participants immediately begin bathing. A few others start the crucial fire under the general guidance of the Muskrat.

The fire must be large. We make it in a rock fireplace, starting with dry spruce twigs and branches, later adding larger and larger pieces of spruce, white pine, juniper, bristlecone pine, and, finally, piñon. After the largest pieces of piñon have burned to glowing coals, a grate is placed on rock supports.

Before starting the meat, Muskrat throws a handful of juniper berries into the fire. Then he lays out generous pieces of elk, cut into strips, lightly peppered, and coated with Wild Barbeque Sauce (page 112). When the sauce begins to burn, each piece is ready to eat. Elk generally requires ⅓ the cooking time of good beef. On the side, Muskrat sautés whole chantarelle mushrooms with olive oil in a cast iron skillet.

Then it's time for Muskrat and the other firebuilders and cooks to slip into the hot spring, where they eat first, served by their loyal and grateful companions. Vice Grips are clamped onto the hot bone ends of the elk to serve as handles, and feasters bounce or float comfortably in the hot mineral water as they eat.

PAN-BROILED ELK BURGERS

Ground elk is best on its own rather than mixed with other meats. Pure ground elk has a tendency to crumble and fall apart when cooked, so your burgers may not come out looking like the hamburgers you're used to. They will taste better.

    1 pound elk, ground

    1 egg, beaten

    1 tablespoon Ground Cherry Sauce (page 102) (*or* Parp's Wild Chutney [page 103])

    ½ teaspoon peppergrass seeds

    ⅓ cup wild rice flour

    2 tablespoons olive oil (*or* corn oil)

Combine ground elk, beaten egg, Ground Cherry Sauce, and peppergrass seeds. Blend well with hands. Add flour.

Form ground elk mixture into patties about ¾ inch thick.

Heat oil in a heavy skillet. Oil should lightly cover the bottom of the skillet.

Place burger patties in very thin hot oil. Brown both sides over medium-high heat. Serve immediately.

ELK AND BEAR HASH

A hunter who is skillful and fortunate enough to bring home both a bear and an elk in one season is sure of one thing: a very large stock of meat. Hash recipes are intended to make the best use of leftover hams and roasts, and this recipe may be adapted to almost any combination of meats. Elk and bear do combine exceptionally well.

> 2 pounds bear meat, cubed
>
> 2 pounds raw potatoes, peeled and cubed
>
> 4 cups Wild Game Brown Sauce (page 104)
>
> 1 pound wild mushrooms, sliced
>
> 2 pounds elk meat, cubed
>
> ¼ teaspoon garlic powder
>
> ½ teaspoon black pepper, freshly ground
>
> ⅛ teaspoon basil

Place bear meat and potatoes in a large saucepan. Cover with Wild Game Brown Sauce and simmer for 20 minutes.

Add mushrooms. Cover and simmer 10 more minutes.

Add elk meat and heat. Do not boil. When thoroughly heated, add remaining ingredients. Heat through.

Serve on toast topped with a poached egg.

Yield: *4 – 6 servings*

VENISON AND WILD RICE STEW

This is a traditional recipe found in various forms throughout North America. It may be prepared with any venison or with similar meats such as antelope, mountain sheep, or lean buffalo.

3   tablespoons olive oil

3   pounds venison, cut in chunks

6   cups hot water

2   cups hot Wild Vegetable Stock (page 77)

2   yellow onions, quartered

¼   teaspoon garlic powder

½   teaspoon peppergrass seeds

1½   cups wild rice, rinsed

Heat oil in a large skillet. Brown some of the meat lightly in the hot oil. Remove. Brown remaining meat.

Place browned venison in a stew pot. Add water, Wild Vegetable Stock, and onions. Simmer very gently, uncovered, for 2 – 3 hours.

Add garlic powder, peppergrass seeds, and wild rice. Cover and simmer for 20 minutes.

Remove cover. Stir. Simmer another 5 minutes. Serve with hot rye bread.

Yield: *6 servings*

NORTH
AMERICAN
BIG
GAME

VENISON STEW
WITH PARP'S DUMPLINGS

    2 tablespoons corn oil

2 – 3 pounds venison for stew

    2 cups lima beans, cooked

    1 teaspoon peppergrass seeds (*or* tarragon)

    2 wild onions, quartered

    3 potatoes, cut in pieces

    4 wild carrots, cut in pieces

    1 cup hot Wild Vegetable Stock (page 77)

hot water to cover

    2 cups stewed tomatoes (*or* ground cherries)

    ¼ teaspoon garlic powder

arrowroot (optional)

Parp's Dumplings (page 308)

Heat oil in a large skillet. Lightly brown venison pieces.

Place venison and lima beans in a pot. Add peppergrass seeds, onions, potatoes, and carrots. Cover with Wild Vegetable Stock and water. Simmer for 2 – 3 hours.

Add tomatoes and garlic powder. Simmer an additional 30 minutes. Thicken, if necessary, with arrowroot.

Prepare Parp's Dumplings. Drop by spoonfuls into the hot stew. Simmer uncovered until the dumplings are done, about 15 minutes. Serve immediately.

Yield: *6 servings*

CREEDE HARGRAVES' GREEN CHILI-VENISON STEW

Creede Hargraves is a high rider of the New West, a man who wanders from the Yucatan Peninsula to the Aleutian Islands. His friends are always pleased to see him after a few months of hard work in the far North or a winter of spearfishing in the Caribbean. His visits may be highlighted by this wonderful stew.

     3 tablespoons rendered bear fat (*or* oil)
     1 clove garlic, chopped
     2 pounds trimmed venison, cut for stew
     3 wild onions, chopped
    1½ pounds green chili strips, chopped
4 or 5 dried jalapeño peppers
     ½ cup wild rice flour
    1½ cups cold water
     2 tablespoons lemon juice

Heat bear fat in a large skillet. Add garlic, venison, and onions. Simmer together for 30 minutes.

Place in a stew pot or Crock-Pot. Add green chilies, jalapeño peppers, and water to cover. Simmer 3 hours.

Place flour in a jar. Add water, cover tightly, and shake well to combine. Strain and stir into stew to thicken. Simmer an additional 15 minutes. Add lemon juice.

Serve with tortillas or use the stew to smother bean burritoes.

Yield: *6 servings*

NORTH AMERICAN BIG GAME

SPICED VENISON

3–5	pounds venison loin (*or* rump)
¼	cup safflower oil (*or* other light oil)
3	wild onions, sliced
1	quart Wild Herb Vinegar (page 68)
1	bay leaf
1	teaspoon ground cinnamon
1	teaspoon allspice (*or* spicebush)
1	teaspoon cloves
1	tablespoon lemon juice
1	teaspoon peppergrass seeds
2	cups stock
2	wild onions, chopped
6	wild carrots, cut in pieces
2	cups wild celery stalks, chopped
½	teaspoon paprika

Rub roast well with safflower oil. Place in a large earthenware bowl or crock and blanket with layers of sliced onion. Pour on Wild Herb Vinegar to cover. Add bay leaf, spices, lemon juice, and peppergrass seeds. Refrigerate for at least 24 hours. The longer the better.

Drain roast and reserve the marinade. Preheat oven to 275°F. Strain marinade and discard vegetables.

Place the venison in a roasting pan. Heat it enough to produce steam when marinade is added. Test by dropping in marinade by the spoonful.

When pan and venison are hot enough, pour in 2 cups of the reserved marinade and 2 cups stock. Cover and roast for 2 hours.

Combine chopped wild onions, carrots, and celery. Sprinkle with paprika, and steam over medium heat for 20 minutes. Add to roast 15 minutes before it is done. Serve with cooked cabbage or steamed amaranth leaves.

Yield: *6 servings*

PAN-BROILED VENISON STEAKS

Venison steaks are not nearly as fat as beef but they still contain enough moisture for pan broiling without additional oil. Venison steaks are only good when eaten very rare.

- 1 2-inch venison steak per person
- ½ teaspoon peppergrass seeds per steak
- salt

Place a steel or iron skillet over high heat. Get it very hot.

Rub each room-temperature steak with peppergrass seeds. Sprinkle a small amount of salt over the bottom of the hot skillet.

Lay in the steaks. Sear each side for 2 or 3 minutes. Reduce heat to medium and cook 2 or 3 minutes longer. Do not overcook. Spill out excess liquid as it appears.

Serve immediately with tossed salad.

VENISON POT ROAST

This fine, moist-heat recipe will tame the toughest old venison. It will also add wonderful flavor to tender meat.

- 3 **pounds venison rump (*or* brisket)**
- 1 **clove garlic, cut**
- ½ **cup wild rice flour**
- 2 **tablespoons corn oil**
- 3 **wild carrots, chopped**
- ½ **cup wild celery stalks, chopped**
- ½ **cup bell pepper, chopped**
- 2 **wild onions, sliced**
- 2 **cups hot stock**
- 1 **teaspoon peppergrass seeds**
- ½ **teaspoon coltsfoot ash**
- ¾ **cup yogurt, warmed**

Preheat oven to 300°F.

Rub trimmed meat with garlic and dust with flour.

Heat oil in a large, heavy oven-proof pot. Brown the meat in the hot oil. Add carrots, celery, bell pepper, sliced onions, and stock.

Cover and cook for 2 hours. Check and turn meat often. Add hot stock as needed.

Remove venison and vegetables. Add peppergrass seeds and coltsfoot ash to the pot liquid. Stir in yogurt just before serving.

Yield: *6 – 8 servings*

BELL PEPPERS
STUFFED WITH VENISON

---

    8 bell peppers

    3 cups venison, cooked and diced

    8 large chantarelle mushrooms, cut in chunks

    3 green onions, cut and sliced

    4 tablespoons olive oil

    1 teaspoon lemon juice

    ¼ teaspoon tarragon

Preheat oven to 325°F.

Clean and remove the cores from the bell peppers. Chop the cores and combine with the venison, mushrooms, onions, olive oil, lemon juice, and tarragon.

Stuff the peppers with the venison mixture. Place stuffed peppers in a shallow baking dish. Bake for 45 – 60 minutes, or until the peppers are tender.

Yield: *4 servings*

NORTH
AMERICAN
BIG
GAME

BAKED VENISON RIBS
WITH WILD RICE STUFFING

This dinner may be legendary in the civilized world but it is very real in the wilderness settlements of the far North and the West. It turns up most often when a well-to-do trader wishes to impress a buyer from the city. It is definitely not camp fare. The recipe will work well with the ribs of any large-game animal. Domestic ribs are too fat and greasy.

½ cup olive oil

5 pounds venison ribs, cut in large serving pieces

6 wild carrots, cut in large pieces

6 potatoes, quartered

1 cup wild celery stalks, chopped

1 cup hot Dark Game Stock (page 72)

4 cups Wild Rice Stuffing (page 108)

Heat about 3 tablespoons of the oil in a skillet. Brown the ribs lightly and quickly.

Place the browned ribs in a Dutch oven or deep roasting pan. Brush with remaining oil.

Place carrots, potatoes, and celery around ribs. Add ½ cup of the Dark Game Stock. Bake uncovered for 45 minutes.

Remove from oven and smother with Wild Rice Stuffing.

Add remaining Dark Game Stock. Cover tightly and bake 45 minutes longer.

Yield: *6 servings*

VENISON MEAT LOAF

1½ pounds venison, ground

3 tablespoons corn oil

1 egg, lightly beaten

¼ cup chantarelle mushrooms, diced

¼ cup wild rice, cooked

1 green onion, finely chopped

1 tablespoon lemon juice

¼ teaspoon cayenne pepper

1 cup warm Dark Game Stock (page 72)

Preheat oven to 375°F.

Combine all ingredients except stock and knead together well. Place the mixture in a lightly oiled loaf pan and shape into a loaf.

Bake for 20 minutes. Cover with Dark Game Stock and return to oven. Bake, basting frequently, for an additional 25 minutes. Serve with Parp's Ground Cherry Sauce (page 102).

Yield: *8 − 10 servings*

BEAR ROAST

 1 bear loin (*or* ham *or* shoulder)

 ½ cup corn oil

 3 wild onions, sliced

 3 cups Wild Herb Vinegar (page 68)

 1 clove garlic, cut

 ½ teaspoon sage

 1 teaspoon tarragon

 ¼ teaspoon rosemary

 ¼ teaspoon thyme

 ½ cup wild rice flour

 ½ cup hot Dark Game Stock (page 72)

 4 sweet potatoes, peeled and steamed

 1 cup Wild Applesauce (page 338)

Rub the cleaned bear meat with corn oil. Place in an
earthenware bowl or crock and cover with sliced onions.
Add Wild Herb Vinegar and refrigerate for 12–24
hours.

Remove roast from marinade and allow to reach room
temperature.

Preheat oven to 450°F. Rub warm roast with cut garlic.
Combine sage, tarragon, rosemary, thyme, and flour.
Dust the roast with this mixture.

Place roast on a rack in a large roasting pan. Place in
hot oven and reduce heat to 325°F. Roast uncovered

about 25 minutes to the pound. Occasionally add small amounts of Dark Game Stock. Roast until internal temperature reaches 180°F.

About 45 minutes before the roast is done, add peeled and steamed sweet potatoes. Ten minutes before removing roast from oven, spread it with Wild Applesauce.

Allow roast to cool at room temperature for about 20 minutes. Serve with more Wild Applesauce, fruit juice, and Acorn Spoon Bread (page 302).

Yield: 4 – 6 servings

DEER AND BEAR PIE

¼ cup corn oil

½ pound deer meat, cubed

½ pound bear meat, cubed

3 cups hot Dark Game Stock (page 72)

1 teaspoon lemon juice

¼ teaspoon paprika

¼ teaspoon ground cloves

1 bay leaf

¼ cup wild celery stalks, chopped

½ cup wild onions, chopped

1 raw potato, diced

½ cup yogurt

pastry for 1 pie crust

milk for glaze

Preheat oven to 450°F.

Heat ½ the oil in a large skillet. Brown the deer meat. Remove. Heat more oil and brown the bear meat. Replace deer meat and add remaining oil. Stir and heat together.

Add Dark Game Stock, lemon juice, paprika, cloves, and bay leaf. Simmer together for about 10 minutes.

Remove bay leaf. Add celery, onions, and potato and heat almost to boiling. Reduce heat and simmer 10 more minutes. Stir in yogurt.

Pour mixture into a pie tin. Cover with pie crust dough, slit crust, and glaze with milk, and bake for 25 minutes.

Yield: *6 − 8 servings*

BEAR BRISKET WITH SAUERKRAUT

4   **pounds bear brisket meat**

½   **cup corn oil**

3   **cups Wild Herb Vinegar (page 68)**

3   **wild onions, sliced**

3   **tablespoons corn oil**

½   **cup wild onions, chopped**

1   **teaspoon peppergrass seeds**

2   **pounds sauerkraut**

1   **cup hot Dark Game Stock (page 72)**

1   **tablespoon lemon juice**

Place bear meat in an earthenware bowl or crock. Cover with ½ cup oil, then add vinegar and sliced onions. Refrigerate 12–24 hours.

Remove roast from marinade and allow to reach room temperature. Discard marinade and onions.

Heat 3 tablespoons oil in a large pot. Lightly brown the chopped onions in the hot oil.

Sprinkle bear meat with peppergrass seeds and brown lightly on both sides. Reduce heat. Smother bear meat with sauerkraut.

Add Dark Game Stock and lemon juice. Cover tightly and simmer for 2 hours. Serve with fruit salad.

Yield: *4–6 servings*

bear

BEAR POT ROAST WITH FRUIT

- 1 4- to 5-pound bear loin (*or* rump *or* shoulder roast)
- ½ cup corn oil
- 3 cups Wild Herb Vinegar (page 68)
- 3 wild onions, sliced
- 3 tablespoons corn oil
- 1 teaspoon peppergrass seeds
- 1 teaspoon lemon juice
- ½ cup wild onions, chopped
- ½ cup wild carrots, diced
- 1 cup hot Dark Game Stock (page 72)
- 3 tablespoons honey
- 1 clove garlic, minced
- 1 cup boiling water
- 1 pound mixed, dried wild fruit
- 3 tablespoons rye flour
- 1 cup cold water

Rub bear meat with ½ cup corn oil. Place in an earthenware bowl or crock. Cover with Wild Herb Vinegar and sliced onions. Refrigerate for 12−24 hours.

Remove roast from marinade and allow to reach room temperature.

Heat 3 tablespoons corn oil in a Dutch oven. Brown meat in hot oil. Sprinkle with peppergrass seeds and lemon juice.

Add chopped onions, carrots, Dark Game Stock, honey, and garlic. Cover tightly and simmer for 2 hours.

Pour boiling water over dried fruit and let stand for 1 hour. Drain and reserve liquid.

When meat has simmered 1 hour, smother with fruit, cover tightly, and finish cooking.

Remove roast from pan and skim the surface of the liquid carefully. Add reserved liquid.

Combine flour and water. Stir into pot liquid and cook until it thickens. Serve this sauce over individual portions of the roast.

Yield: *4 −6 servings*

NORTH AMERICAN BIG GAME

VENISON MARROW

Venison marrow is exceedingly nutritious and un-forgettably delicious. It will make you happy that you made the effort to pack out the bones with the meat.

POACHED VENISON MARROW

¼ cup Dark Game Stock (page 72)

4 − 6 ½-inch slices of marrow

In a shallow pan, heat the Dark Game Stock to boiling. The stock should scarcely cover the bottom of the pan.

Reduce heat to a simmer. Lay in the marrow slices and poach gently for 1½ minutes. Do not turn. Do not overcook. Serve at once as hors d'oeuvres on toast, or with poached eggs and toast for breakfast.

BAKED VENISON MARROW

Preheat oven to 325°F.

Cut marrow bones into pieces about 4 inches long.

Place on a baking sheet and bake for 20 − 30 minutes. Serve with long spoons.

Yield: *4 − 6 servings*

SAUTÉED LIVER

This recipe is suitable for the livers of most large game including deer, elk, and bear. We never have enough venison livers for our own satisfaction because of a local tradition to which we happily conform. This tradition requires that we donate at least half of our liver to Pappy Fairchild, a man who pioneered in our area. Pappy, however, doesn't bother to cook his liver before eating it and would be shocked at such a recipe.

- 1 pound big-game liver
- ½ teaspoon black pepper
- ½ cup rye flour
- 3 tablespoons corn oil
- 1 teaspoon lemon juice

Clean liver and slice into serving pieces about ¾ inch thick.

Combine pepper and flour. Dredge liver slices in this mixture until fully coated.

Heat the corn oil in a skillet over medium heat. Sauté liver slices until each side is lightly browned. Turn once only and do not overcook. Sprinkle with lemon juice.

Serve with homemade catsup or Ground Cherry Sauce (page 102).

Yield: *4 servings*

GRILLED ELK HEART

Most elk fanciers agree that the heart is the best portion, and a true delicacy. Many say that cooking an elk heart ruins the taste and texture of the meat; overcooking surely does.

- 1 **elk heart**
- 2 **wild onions, sliced**
- 1 **cup olive oil**

Rinse and clean heart under cold running water. Split and remove membranes and arteries.

Slice the heart into 1-inch slices. Place in a dish or bowl sandwiched between slices of onion. Cover with olive oil.

Refrigerate for 5 days. Rearrange slices daily to prevent drying.

To cook, heat a small amount of olive oil in a heavy skillet. Grill elk heart slices over medium heat until lightly browned on both sides. Serve with steamed wild green vegetables.

Yield: *4 servings*

SAUTÉED BRAINS

Brains of venison—either deer, elk, caribou, or moose—are for some hunters the ultimate delicacy. They must be cleaned and cooked carefully.

       4   tablespoons Wild Herb Vinegar (page 68)
       1   gallon cold water
    1 – 2   pounds of venison
       1   quart boiling water
       ⅓   cup white cornmeal (*or* acorn meal)
       2   tablespoons safflower oil
       1   teaspoon lemon juice
       ¼   teaspoon paprika
       1   tablespoon parsley, chopped

Add 2 tablespoons of Wild Herb Vinegar to the cold water in a large bowl. Soak the brains in this for 2 hours.

Skin the brains, if necessary, and clean them under cold running water. Remove all membranes.

Place brains in boiling water. Add remaining vinegar. Simmer for 3 – 5 minutes. Remove, dry, and dust with cornmeal.

Heat oil in a skillet and sauté brains on 1 side for 2 minutes. Turn. Sprinkle with lemon juice and paprika. Sauté for another minute. Remove and garnish with parsley. Serve with poached eggs and Parp's Wild Chutney (page 103).

Yield: *4 servings*

KIDNEY STEW

  1 venison kidney, cut for stew

  2 tablespoons Wild Herb Vinegar (page 68)

  3 tablespoons olive oil

  1 pound venison neck (*or* shoulder meat), cut
     for stew

1½ wild onions, chopped

  4 wild carrots, cut in pieces

  3 potatoes, cut in pieces

  3 cups Dark Game Stock (page 72)

  ½ teaspoon tarragon

  ⅛ teaspoon thyme

  ⅛ teaspoon savory

  ⅛ teaspoon marjoram

  1 tablespoon lemon juice

  3 tablespoons cornstarch

  ½ cup cold water

Clean and wash kidney in cold running water. Combine
with Wild Herb Vinegar in a bowl.

Heat oil in a large pot. Lightly brown the venison stew
meat in the hot oil. Do not brown kidney meat.

Add onions, carrots, and potatoes and sauté for 10
minutes. Add stock. Simmer, covered, for 1 hour.

Add herbs and lemon juice. Combine cornstarch and
water and use this mixture to thicken the stew.

Drain and add kidney pieces. Simmer over low heat, tightly covered, for 20 minutes. Serve with biscuits.

Yield: *4 servings*

SIMMERED ELK TONGUE

The tongue of any member of the venison group is edible. An elk tongue is very large and will provide enough meat for several people. It is also delicious sliced cold for sandwiches. The best tongue comes from young spike or club elk. It is better than the best beef tongue.

1 3- to 4-pound fresh tongue

2 wild onions

2 wild carrots

2 ribs wild celery

boiling water to cover

Scrub tongue carefully. Do not attempt to skin raw.

Place tongue, onions, carrots, and celery in a pot. Cover with water and simmer, uncovered, for 2 hours.

Remove and drain tongue. Cool tongue under water just enough to handle it comfortably. Skin the tongue, then return it to the hot liquid for 10 minutes.

You may now serve the tongue hot or allow it to cool slowly and completely in the cooking liquid. Serve hot with boiled potatoes and beets or serve cold, sliced diagonally, for sandwiches.

Yield: *4 servings*

CHAPTER ELEVEN

COOKED WILD VEGETABLES AND GREENS

This chapter treats those edible wild plants that are best cooked and used as potherbs or as cooked vegetables. In many cases, wild vegetables are comparable in taste to our accustomed domestic greens and roots. Their flavors vary from palatable to bitter and from bland to pungent. Each fancier of wild edibles soon develops groups of tastes that are compatible, mixing the bland plants with spicier ones to create the desired effect.

We often refer to blanching as a means of reducing a bitter or wild taste. Blanching involves covering the living plant with a basket for several days, thereby greatly diminishing the amount of sunlight the plant absorbs and causing the stems and leaves to become longer and lose their color. Blanching plants to a light yellow or white color also often eliminates the necessity of boiling all the nutrients out in two or more waters.

Many wild vegetables are best when combined with leftover game or fowl. To create such a dish, simply steam or boil any wild green or sliced root according to the recipes in this chapter. Then toss or combine with small slices of wild meat, either cold or heated. The combinations are endless and they always seem to work if you let your imagination go. Cold snake, for example, combines well with a variety of cooked greens—tastes just like chicken, as they say in Georgia.

Amaranth (pigweed). *Amaranthus retroflexus*

This plant is common across North America and is well known as a weed to gardeners and as a food to foragers. It has always been widely used by most Native American groups and was cultivated by many. As a vegetable, fresh young amaranth greens and shoots may be boiled for 10 minutes or steamed for 20 and served as a substitute for a mild spinach dish. The rather bland taste may be spiced with a sprinkling of Wild Herb Vinegar and combined with sliced hard-cooked eggs. Steamed amaranth greens are also excellent when combined with sliced meat from small game. Very young amaranth plants may be chopped and used raw in salads if you prefer a bland green base, but we feel they taste best cooked.

Balsamroot. *Balsamorhiza* spp.

Balsamroot is one of those rare plants that are useful as food throughout the year. In spring, the young plants may be torn into salads or they may be lightly steamed over a mild vinegar solution and served as cooked greens. Later in the year, cover the more mature plants with boiling water for about 8 minutes, then drain and steam until tender, about 25 minutes. Increase both the boiling and the steaming time for very mature plants in late summer and autumn. Through autumn and winter, dig the roots and eat them raw or cooked. They are excellent when baked (350°F, 40 minutes), boiled, sautéed, or included with roasts. They also make good substitutes for parsnips or carrots in any recipe, especially with the addition of a ½ teaspoon of Wild Herb Vinegar or lemon juice.

Bitterroot. *Lewisisa rediviva*

This is a famous food plant used extensively by most Native American groups. In early spring, the root is tender and the taste acceptably mild. It gets considerably more bitter later in the year. To prepare, gather roots early in the spring and remove the outer peel by rubbing the root between the hands. Then bake the root cores at 325°F for 45 minutes, or boil in water to cover until the consistency changes to a gel. Serve as a side dish with honey or lemon juice.

Broad-leaved milkweeds. *Asclepias speciosa* and *A. syriaca*

Asclepias syriaca is the species found in the eastern United States and *A. speciosa* is the one found in the western states and North. Both are broad-leaved milkweeds and are easily distinguished from the very narrow-leaved poison milkweeds (*A. subverticillata* and *A. verticillata*). All narrow-leaved milkweeds should be avoided entirely; no part of any milkweed should be eaten raw. This observed, the broad-leaved milkweed challenges the cattail for the title of "outdoor pantry," for it provides many kinds of foods from its several parts. The young shoots, tender tops of older plants, unopened buds, and hard young seedpods of all broad-leaved milkweeds are edible, nutritious, and delicious if prepared properly. One species, *A. tuberosa*, produces tuberous roots that are also edible, but other milkweed roots are inedible for one reason or another. Milkweed is a plant that can carry us through a long season. The young shoots appear through spring and early summer. They are best when they're about six inches tall (four inches in harsh

climates). The shoots, and all other parts of milkweed, should first be placed in boiling water for three minutes, then drained and steamed, or prepared according to any recipe for asparagus. Steamed until very tender, the shoots are as palatable as any wild or domestic vegetable. Later in the summer, after the shoots have matured, either the leaves or the top-most parts of the plants may be gathered.

These may be prepared according to any recipe for mustard greens, except that they must first be covered with boiling water for three minutes and drained. Still later in the season, the unopened flower buds can be covered with boiling water for three minutes, drained, covered for another five minutes, drained, and then cooked according to any recipe for green beans. These same instructions apply to the hard green seed pods which appear later, usually after the flower buds have opened. After boiling in the two waters, treat the pods as large vegetables. Even those milkweed parts which are too mature and tough to make good eating have a use. If they are chopped into sections and boiled in two waters like the buds, you can include them in small-game stews, casseroles, and roasts as a tenderizer for stringy meats. For a time, some modern authorities charged that this Native American use was unfounded. Recent evidence proves that milkweed does indeed possess meat tenderizing properties and that it is high in asclepain, an excellent and harmless tenderizer.

Since broad-leaved milkweed resembles the poisonous dogbanes, one should learn the difference between the two before collecting.

Broad-leaf plantain (Indian wheat, plantain).
Plantago major

Young plantain leaves, with stems removed, may be steamed for about 20 minutes over water combined with a teaspoon of Wild Herb Vinegar, or generally treated in the same way as spinach. Plantain is plentiful in most areas, when in season, and may be used in quantity. Its taste is vaguely reminiscent of mushrooms and it makes a good potherb for stews, soups, and casseroles. Steamed plantain leaves make a fine breakfast, especially when served with soft-boiled eggs, venison sausage or meatballs, and wild rice or acorn cakes.

Bulrush (tule). *Scirpus* spp.

Bulrush, like cattail and milkweed, is widespread and provides several kinds of food all-year-round. The three plants, often found very near each other, would be ample food to prevent starvation in a survival situation. Indeed, a family of individualists could easily make all their meals of vegetables and breads gathered from these plants and would need only an occasional patch of berries or a mess of fish to avoid boredom. Bulrush, like all aquatic or semiaquatic plants, should either be gathered in areas that are free of pollution, or treated with a purifying solution before cooking. All roots of bulrush are edible all-year-round and may be eaten raw in salads or baked, boiled, or dried for use as flour or meal. At the base of the long stems one finds, under the outer layer, a fine heart of almost pure starch. The heart is sweet, crisp, and delicious eaten raw, or steamed very lightly and left unseasoned. In early spring the bulrush sends up raw shoots which you can cook like as-

paragus. These shoots often reappear in autumn, when they seem to taste even better. Both the pollen and the seeds may be used to make a flour or meal which is especially good when mixed with cattail pollen, acorn meal, or any meal made from wild seeds with a more pronounced taste.

Burdock. *Arctium minus* and *A. lappa*

Burdock is most commonly encountered as an ingredient in sukiyaki and other Asian dishes. It is cultivated in some European areas and in Japan but its strong taste has inhibited its popular use in this country. It is often listed as a salad plant and if you can tolerate its strong taste raw it is worth a try. It's best as a cooked green or as a cooked root. For these purposes, gather only the youngest shoots and plants, preferably blanched for at least five days. To cook the greens, first cover the plant with boiling water to which a tablespoon of lemon juice is added. Then drain and steam above water containing a teaspoon of Wild Herb Vinegar. Serve with oil and vinegar or lemon juice, and peppergrass seeds. To cook the roots, first peel them completely and slice them thin, then boil them for 15 minutes in water to cover, with a tablespoon of baking soda. Drain, and boil an additional 15 minutes in water to cover with a teaspoon of Wild Herb Vinegar. Serve brushed with corn oil and sprinkled with peppergrass seeds. Thus prepared, the roots are a very tasty vegetable dish. The young roots may be dug in late spring and summer and stored in a cellar for year-round use.

Cattail. *Typha latifolia*

The cattail is the official "outdoor pantry," known to Boy Scouts and foragers everywhere. Beginners should find it relatively easy to identify in almost any season or condition. It's useful practice for beginners to first identify the plant by its familiar and unmistakable appearance, then locate young shoots as they grow and change. Each new stage will bring added insight. This, incidentally, is the ideal method of learning about all edible wild plants—by slow and accurate observation. When the first new plants appear in early spring, pick them off at the root, peel and eat raw, chop into salads, or cook like asparagus. When the pollen stalks are solid green and quite young, you can pull, prepare, and eat them exactly like corn on the cob. Through early and sometimes mid-summer, the plant produces sprouts. These are white and tender, similar in texture to bean sprouts, and they appear suddenly at the base of the plant and along the root system. They are best eaten raw in salads, but may also be steamed or boiled or included in stews and soups. Serve them warm, but not cooked, on roasts or fowl. Parp says they're best in peanut butter sandwiches. Young rootstocks are also excellent at any time of the year. These should be peeled and eaten raw or boiled or baked. In all cases, the flavor of cattail is delicate and delicious.

Chickweed. *Stellaria media*

Chickweed should be a main part of every forager's diet. It grows everywhere, especially in populated areas, and

young shoots are available through most of the year,
including winter. It tastes mild, but not so bland as to
be unappetizing, and it makes an excellent potherb or
garnish for delicately flavored stews, soups, and poultry
dishes. It is also fine when prepared as a steamed green
and many people prefer it to grocery greens. Steam for
30 minutes above water flavored with a teaspoon of Wild
Herb Vinegar. Serve with lemon wedges or an oil and
vinegar dressing. It's an excellent vegetable to serve
with roast chicken or grouse, or raw in salads.

Chicory. *Cichorium intybus*

Chicory may be difficult to identify before the flowers
appear unless you know from previous seasons where it
grows. For that reason, it is less often used as a food
plant than as a coffee substitute, although the shoots
and young plants are also edible. For best results,
blanch the young preflowering plants for three or four
days, then harvest and use them immediately. Chop
them into sections and boil in water to cover for ten
minutes. Then drain and place in fresh boiling water
which contains a teaspoon of lemon juice. Drain again
and place in a steamer above boiling water which
contains a teaspoon of Wild Herb Vinegar. Steam,
covered, for five minutes and serve hot, brushed lightly
with safflower oil and sprinkled with peppergrass
seeds.

Dandelion. *Taraxacum officinale*

The dandelion is well known as an edible plant and it is
very often the only wild plant that would-be foragers

ever try. Many people, temporarily enthusiastic about the idea of wild foods, go right out and dig the first dandelion they see. Needless to say, the extreme bitterness of mature dandelions is quite enough to convince the dilettante that the grocery store is the only place to gather food. The dandelion is a useful plant for beginners, but only if gathered or dug in the earliest shoot stages, certainly before the blossoms appear. Even then, many experienced foragers do not care for the taste of dandelion and the bitterness must usually be overcome by blanching and by cooking in two waters. Another solution to the problem of bitterness is to dig up the plants and transplant them into boxes in the cellar. The shoots usually appear all winter long and these young, tender, naturally blanched shoots are truly delicious. They may be used raw in salads, or cooked in stews, soups, and roasts, or steamed and served with lemon juice. If your shoots or leaves are not blanched or if they are bitter even though blanched, place the plants in a saucepan and cover with boiling water. Let stand without heat for three minutes. Drain through a colander and repeat, adding a teaspoon of Wild Herb Vinegar to the second water. After this preparation, the plants may be used in any appropriate recipe. They are best when scraped, cut into pieces, and cooked in stews or with moist meats.

Evening primrose. *Oenothera biennis*

In Europe evening primrose is cultivated for food use, and the leaves and shoots are used in salads. However, we find the okra-shaped young pods to be much tastier. To cook these, gather them while they're hard and green and keep them for one week before cooking. Then

cover with boiling water, let stand for several minutes, and drain. Repeat twice, then place the pods on a rack in a vegetable steamer. Sprinkle with lemon juice, and steam, covered tightly, for 25 minutes or until tender. Serve as a vegetable or combine with a sweet-tasting root or tuber such as cicely. Some species have thick roots which we boil in three waters and eat with cinnamon and honey.

Fireweed. *Epilobium angustifolium*

This well-known plant loves waste places and burned-out areas all over North America and Europe. It is especially plentiful in our Rocky Mountain region and we are quite familiar with it. This is a plant you should find easy to locate and identify. It's almost impossible to mistake with the aid of a field guide. Young shoots are the only practical food element and you can eat them steamed, boiled, or in soups and stews. The pith of young or mature fireweed stems is also edible. Chop it and use it as you would beans or include it in soups and stews as a thickener.

Ground cherry (strawberry tomato).
Physalis spp.

All of the yellow flowered *Physalis* species produce excellent berries. The ground cherry is mentioned frequently in this book because it is a versatile substitute for many domestic ingredients. Use it raw or cooked to replace tomatoes in salads, stews, soups, sauces, and casseroles. Use it raw or cooked to replace berries in any recipe calling for strawberries, gooseberries, blackberries, or cherries. It makes excellent catsups and chutneys as well as pies, jams, and preserves. This has always been a favorite food of many Native American groups, and was probably cultivated by several. It is abundant and widespread and may be stewed, mashed, canned, bottled, dried, or frozen for year-round use. It should only be gathered when ripe or, at least, after falling. The berries frequently fall to the ground before they are ripe and remain in their distinctive husks where they are well protected. Some varieties burst open the husks as they ripen. If ground cherries are gathered after falling but before they are fully ripe, they may be held until ripe and will keep in their husks for long periods.

Jerusalem Artichoke (sunchoke). *Helianthus tuberosus*

One of the most versatile and palatable of all tubers, Jerusalem artichoke may be dug and eaten any time in autumn or winter and is usually quite abundant in areas where it occurs at all. Chokes are widely distributed over North America, and have always been used by Native American groups. The tubers contain few calories and are very high in thiamin, potassium, and other vitamins and minerals. Sauté, steam, boil, mash, or bake them. Ground chokes are an excellent extender for meat or vegetable loafs or wild game pies.

Lamb's-quarters, goosefoot.
Chenopodium spp.

Either of these plants, gathered young and in quantity, is excellent when prepared in the same way as spinach, either boiled or steamed. If the plants are to be steamed, they should first be covered with boiling water to which a teaspoon of lemon juice is added. Let them sit without heat for 3 or 4 minutes, then drain thoroughly and steam, tightly covered, for about 30 to 35 minutes. Serve with lemon juice or oil and vinegar.

Mustard. *Brassica* spp.

Mustard, says Parp, must have originated on Olympus under the cultivation of the same refined gods who invented poetry, drama, and music. It surely is an exquisite wild food, tasty and versatile. Mustard greens have long been known as superior and, of course, the seeds offer one of the finest seasonings available (see Mustard Sauce, page 104). All species of *Brassica* are edible, although some produce more tender greens than others. Mustard greens may be gathered and used throughout the season, making them one of the most available of all wild greens. To prepare, remove and reserve the seeds, then chop the leaves and tender stems into sections and place on a rack in a vegetable steamer. Add a teaspoon of Wild Herb Vinegar to the boiling water and steam, covered tightly, for about 30 minutes. Reserve water for stock.

Pond lily (waterlily). *Nuphar polysepalum*

This plant is best collected in mid- to late summer, when so many others are past their prime. The seeds make good popcorn (see page 341). The roots or tubers have a high starch content and are sweet and appetizing. To prepare the tubers, first place them in boiling water for 20 minutes. Then drain and peel them to expose the inner core. The cores may then be steamed for 10 minutes before eating with yogurt, or they may be used in soups, stews, or soufflés. Both seeds and tuber cores are useful as flour or meal when dried and ground together.

Purslane. *Portulaca oleracea*

Purslane is so commonly regarded as a weed that many gardeners are astonished to learn that it is edible. Yet it is one of the finest and most versatile of wild edibles and has long been used in Europe. A cinch to identify, young purslane plants are available from spring through fall. New plants usually emerge after rains late in the season. Young plants should be cut off at ground level, washed, and steamed for 25 minutes. They may be cooked and served much as spinach or other greens and are also excellent in meatloafs, soups, and soufflés. Stems may be sun-dried and stored for winter use as a potherb. Try purslane chopped and raw in salads, especially late in the season when many other salad plants are gone.

Salsify (oyster plant). *Tragopogon* spp.

There are several species of salsify, one of which is the common garden variety, *T. porrifolius* or oyster plant. The cultivated variety has a more pronounced oysterlike flavor than the wild species, but all possess this flavor to some degree. Salsify is a fine wild edible and, like many

root foods, it is useful for digging in the winter months. To arrange this, simply locate and identify the plants and mark them with stakes so they may be found in barren months. Then just dig up the roots as you need them. They do not keep well once dug, so plan to use them immediately. Cultivated salsify roots should not be peeled or scraped until just before cooking, although we believe that all wild salsify should definitely be peeled or scraped well before cooking or eating. To prevent discoloring after peeling, add a small amount of lemon juice to the cooking water or brush the peeled roots with a solution of corn oil and lemon juice or vinegar. Salsify may be cooked according to any recipe for carrots or parsnips. The salsify recipes we include in this book apply to all varieties.

Saltbush (orache). *Atriplex* spp.

As you've guessed from its common name, this green shrub contains natural salts that will appeal to many people. Young shoots may be collected in late spring or early summer and, occasionally, even later in the year. Of the several varieties, *A. patula* is the most interesting to foragers because its stems and shoots are tender and juicy. They should be combined with a milder green, such as amaranth, then chopped and steamed for about 20 minutes, or until very tender. Serve with lemon juice or an oil and vinegar dressing.

Snowdrops. *Orogenia fusiformis* and *O. linearifolia*

These small roots are similar to potatoes or other tubers

and may be used in exactly the same ways. They are so delicious that most people like them better than potatoes. Bake them with the skins on for about 15 minutes at 350°F for a small baking sheet full. Try steaming together one part yampa root, one part Indian potato, and one part nut grass tubers for 20 minutes (large tubers should be sliced). Serve sprinkled with corn oil and coltsfoot ash as a side dish with roast bear, small game, or trout.

Springbeauty (fairy spuds). *Claytonia* spp.

Older springbeauty plants have the largest corms, often over an inch in diameter. They make delicious vegetables. To cook, first peel and wash thoroughly, then boil as potatoes for about 30 minutes. Some species of *Claytonia* are found nearly everywhere. Alpine springbeauty, for example, grows in our Rocky Mountain neighborhood at elevations exceeding 10,000 feet. For other uses, refer to the entry in Chapter Three.

Stinging nettle (nettle). *Urtica* spp.

The nettle is another wild plant that is important in French cooking. Use leather gloves to gather young shoots about six inches tall, blanched if possible. With a scissors, cut the shoots into two-inch segments and place them in a saucepan with boiling water to cover. Let stand for 5 minutes, then drain and steam for 20 minutes. Serve with wilted or steamed mustard greens or as spinach. If you dig nettle roots in the fall and transplant them indoors to a cool, dark space, they will produce blanched shoots all winter.

Sweet cicely (sweetroot). *Osmorhiza obtusa*

Sweet cicely is commonly used as a flavoring and for that alone it is valuable. The roots have an aniselike taste that varies in strength from quite mild to very strong. Stronger specimens, including those gathered late in the year, should be reserved for flavoring baked goods and wild brews such as chicory. Mild cicely roots make excellent eating; best found in May and June, they should be set in the sun for two hours, then boiled in scant water and peeled.

Sweet clover (red clover). *Trifolium pratense*

Sweet clover may be steamed in a large mass for 15 minutes, then combined with any other cooked green to add protein and other nutrients. Dry the blossoms and use them in soups and stews.

Tansy-mustard. *Descurainia* spp.

Tansy-mustard greens are excellent and may be steamed like other mustard greens, wilted (see Wilted Amaranth Greens, page 268), or used as a potherb in stews, soups, and soufflés. Tansy-mustard is safe in normal quantities but should not be eaten in excess or over long periods of time. To steam the young plants, tear them into three- or four-inch pieces and place in a rack over boiling water. Cover and steam 20 minutes, then remove the plants, place them in a colander, and rinse under cold running water. Discard first steaming water, replace with fresh water, and steam the plants again, covered, for about 15 minutes.

Vetch (wild pea). *Vicia* spp.

Pick wild pea pods when they are very young and use them in exactly the same way as domestic pea pods, especially in Asian cooking. All wild peas should be cooked before eating. Either add them to stews or casseroles, or steam them for ten minutes or until very tender.

Wappato (arrowhead). *Sagittaria latifolia*

Use a potato fork 'cause they're way down in the mud. They are surely worth gathering in late autumn, however, as they are among the finest of tubers. All arrowheads produce tubers in varying size and texture. They may be boiled, baked, or used in stews, soups, and roasts. They are best stored for a month or more before baking. They may be peeled after cooking, or sun-dried after boiling. Dried, they will keep indefinitely.

Watercress. *Nasturtium officinale*

Watercress is probably the oldest known and longest used wild edible. It is an essential ingredient in French cooking. Its use in salads is well known, but as a potherb it is without compare. It grows wild throughout most of North America and the world and may be gathered even in winter in some areas. Its spicy, pungent taste is a welcome break from the blandness so common among wild edibles, and it is a valuable ingredient in many cooked dishes, especially stews, soups, and moist roasts. Since a little goes a long way in such dishes, keeping excess watercress fresh and crisp is often a problem. To do so, tie it loosely in small bunches and place these in glass containers large enough to avoid crowding the cress. Add an inch or so of fresh, cold water to each container and store in the refrigerator. Change the water frequently, about once a week. To use, rinse, shake dry, and cut away any tough or rubbery ends. Chopped watercress is an excellent garnish for almost all soups. It is also excellent when steamed very lightly and served with steamed wild rice.

Wild asparagus (asparagus). *Asparagus officinalis*

Here it is, the wild plant that isn't wild. There are, of course, several other plants in the wild and in the garden that appear identical to asparagus, but they don't taste like it, unless your taste buds are aroused by the fact of wildness and by the mild effort of gathering the plants. In any case, wild asparagus is easy to locate, easy to identify, easy to gather, easy to cook, and easy to eat. Use any asparagus recipe and don't "boil in two waters." Cook as little as possible, just until tender. Serve with lemon juice.

Wild cabbage (squaw cabbage). *Caulanthus crassicaulis*

Wild cabbage is much more bitter than the domestic variety, but there is little difference otherwise. Because of the bitterness, however, wild cabbage requires pre-cooking. It must be boiled in water, not steamed, then rinsed in cold water and boiled again. These steps must sometimes be repeated four or five times if the cabbage is excessively bitter or mature. Young leaves are best, gathered in mid-spring and blanched, if possible.

Wild caraway (swamproot, yampa).
Perideridia spp.

These roots should be dug in autumn and stored in a pantry or root cellar. They keep well and may be used throughout the year. To preserve the marvelous flavor of wild caraway roots, they should be cooked as little as possible. We recommend steaming them for about 20 minutes, or including them with a roast for the last 35 or 40 minutes. Please check Index for other recipes as well as the entry in Chapter Three.

Wild carrot (Queen Anne's lace, carrot weed).
Daucus carota

Caution: Because of its resemblance to deadly poison-ous plants, the wild carrot is extremely dangerous for

beginners. See our entry in Chapter Three for more information and please do not pick any wild carrot until you have studied the subject thoroughly and have consulted a competent field guide. One bite may be fatal. On the other hand, we'll assume that you've done your homework and have a nice mess of wild carrot roots. Peel them very lightly with a vegetable peeler and slice them rather thin. Then combine with any small wild starch tuber, such as springbeauty, sweet cicely, or Indian potato, and steam until tender.

Wild onion (nodding onion). *Allium* spp.

Before eating any plant that resembles an onion, be certain you can readily identify the death camas. Also be certain you can readily identify the onion you're after. The general rule is that if it looks, smells, and tastes like onion it is onion, but do be careful. Death camas is aptly named and is likely to be growing with any wild onions. Identify each plant positively and individually. Just as with the domestic onion, either the bulb or the top may be used in soups, stews, and other dishes. Chopped or sliced wild onions may be used exactly like domestic varieties in any recipe.

Wild potato. *Solanum jamesii*

With so many wild starchy tubers and roots readily available, there scarcely seems any need to mention wild potato. But many people are more comfortable gathering and eating wild plants that are similar to the domestic species than they are with wild plants that seem far less familiar. For that reason, we feel obliged to caution against using green wild potatoes of any of the *Solanum* species. As the name implies, all varieties are noted for their high solanine content. Solanine is a toxic alkaloid which, taken in large doses, can cause all sorts of discomfort, difficulty, and even death. Solanine is greatly concentrated in the green skins, sprouts, stems, and flesh of all potatoes, including the domestic variety. For some reason, however, people seem more apt to eat green wild potatoes than green domestic potatoes and so we caution against any such rashness. Some wild potato species also produce berries which are very poisonous. All of this observed, the fully developed and ripened tuber of the wild potato may be used in exactly the same ways as the domestic potato. Incidentally, it is probably wise to avoid eating any potato raw, wild or domestic.

asparagus

STEAMED WILD ASPARAGUS

This procedure works for wild or domestic vegetables, except those that must be boiled in 2 or more waters.

3 cups wild asparagus, washed and cut

lemon juice (optional)

Bring water to boil in the bottom of a vegetable steamer.

Place cut asparagus over, but not in, boiling water. No water should touch asparagus. Steam over medium-high heat until tender. Do not overcook.

Serve with freshly squeezed lemon juice.

PAN-STEAMED WILD ASPARAGUS

2 pounds fresh wild asparagus

½ teaspoon coltsfoot ash

1 lemon, squeezed for juice

1 lemon, cut in wedges (optional)

Wash asparagus under cold running water. Place cold water in a heavy skillet to a depth of about 1 inch.

Place skillet over high heat and bring to a boil. Drop in asparagus, cover, and reduce heat. Simmer until tender, about 6 minutes.

Remove from heat and drain. Place asparagus on a serving dish and sprinkle with lemon juice. Garnish with lemon wedges.

BAKED WILD ASPARAGUS

     1 pound fresh young wild asparagus (*or* similar wild shoots)
    ⅓ cup safflower oil
    ⅓ cup rye flour
     2 tablespoons acorn (*or* cattail) meal
     1 wild onion, diced
    ¼ cup cheddar cheese, grated
     1 teaspoon wild thyme
    ½ teaspoon coltsfoot ash
    ½ teaspoon sorrel leaves, chopped

Preheat oven to 350°F.

Place washed and trimmed wild asparagus in an oiled casserole dish. Pour safflower oil over asparagus.

Combine rye flour and acorn meal. Add remaining ingredients and mix thoroughly.

Pour flour mixture over asparagus. Bake, uncovered, for 40 minutes. Serve hot.

GREENS WITH WILD ONION

> 6 cups wild greens, washed and torn into pieces
>
> 2 tablespoons olive oil
>
> 2 wild onions, sliced
>
> 2 tablespoons Wild Herb Vinegar (page 68)
>
> 1 tablespoon molasses (*or* dark honey)

Greens may first be treated in boiling water with a teaspoon of lemon juice, or they may be fresh. Either way, place greens in a vegetable steamer, cover, and steam briefly.

Heat oil in a skillet. Sauté onion until lightly browned.

Combine vinegar and molasses. Add to onion and mix gently. Add greens and heat through.

GLAZED WILD ONIONS

> 10 – 15 wild onions
>
> ¼ cup corn oil
>
> 4 tablespoons light honey
>
> 1 teaspoon wild mint, chopped

Remove tops and place onions in a vegetable steamer. Cover tightly and steam 20 minutes. Remove outer skins.

Combine oil and honey in a large saucepan and place over low heat until well warmed. Do not burn.

Place skinned and steamed onions in oil/honey mixture. Simmer about 10 minutes, stirring gently.

Pour glazed onions into serving dish. Sprinkle with wild mint and serve with roast lamb, bear, or wild pig.

STEAMED SALSIFY WITH WATERCRESS

2 cups salsify root, scraped and cut in pieces

1 teaspoon Wild Herb Vinegar (page 68)

1 tablespoon olive oil

1 clove garlic, minced

3 tablespoons watercress, chopped

½ teaspoon coltsfoot ash

Place salsify root in a vegetable steamer over water containing Wild Herb Vinegar. Cover tightly and steam until tender, about 10 – 15 minutes.

Heat olive oil in a skillet. Add garlic and watercress. Heat 2 – 3 minutes and combine well.

Add steamed salsify and coltsfoot ash. Simmer 2 – 3 minutes or until heated through. Serve with pot roast, roast bear, or small game.

BAKED SALSIFY

4 cups Wild Vegetable Stock (page 77)

12 – 15 salsify (*or* similar) roots, scrubbed

3 tablespoons safflower oil

2 tablespoons sorrel leaves, chopped

Preheat oven to 350°F.

Bring Wild Vegetable Stock to a boil in a large saucepan over moderate heat. Add salsify roots and boil 10 – 12 minutes. Drain, peel, and slice.

Brush sliced salsify with safflower oil. Place in a shallow baking dish and sprinkle with sorrel. Bake, uncovered, about 30 minutes or until nicely browned. Serve as a vegetable with dinner.

SWEET SALSIFY

½ cup water

½ teaspoon lemon juice

2 cups salsify root, scraped and sliced

¼ cup honey

¼ teaspoon paprika

Bring water and lemon juice to a rapid boil in a medium saucepan.

Add salsify root. Bring water to second boil. Reduce heat and simmer, covered tightly, until tender.

Drain salsify and place in a serving dish. Add honey and combine to coat all pieces. Sprinkle with paprika and serve as a vegetable with dinner. It is especially good with roast bear or small game.

POND LILY TUBERS AND GREENS

1   pound pond lily tubers

2   tablespoons oil

3 – 4   wild onions, diced

1   small bunch wild greens

½   teaspoon peppergrass seeds

¼   teaspoon coltsfoot ash

Place tubers in boiling water for 10 minutes. Hold under cold running water and peel to expose cores.

Place tuber cores in a vegetable steamer. Cover tightly and steam until tender, about 20 minutes.

Heat oil in a heavy skillet and sauté onions until lightly browned. Add greens and sauté briefly.

Place all ingredients in a serving dish. Sprinkle with peppergrass seeds and coltsfoot ash. Serve immediately.

SWEET AND SOUR WILD CABBAGE

Be sure to pick this plant when young. It will not readily adapt to most cabbage recipes because it needs pre-cooking. This recipe provides a practical and tasty side dish that is appropriate with Asian meals or with pot roasts.

  2 kettles boiling water

  2 large bunches wild cabbage leaves

  6 wild onions, chopped

  ½ cup lemon juice

  ¼ cup gooseberries

  ½ cup apple cider

  ¼ cup light honey

  2 tablespoons safflower oil

  ½ cup currants, soaked overnight

  ⅛ teaspoon spicebush

  1 tablespoon wild caraway seeds

Have both kettles of water boiling simultaneously. Rinse wild cabbage leaves well under cold running water, then place in one of the kettles. Boil 3 minutes.

Drain cabbage leaves through colander, discarding first water. Refill kettle and replace over high heat to return to a boil. Hold colander of cabbage leaves under cold running water while squeezing gently.

Place cabbage leaves in second kettle of boiling water. Boil 3 minutes. Repeat the above double boiling.

Place precooked wild cabbage leaves and all other ingredients in a large kettle. Simmer, covered, for 20 minutes. Serve hot with dinner.

caraway

WILTED AMARANTH GREENS

In less wary days, nearly everyone enjoyed the old Southern tradition of eating fresh wild or domestic greens wilted in hot bacon grease. It was an unforgettable taste experience. But forget it we must, for we are now alert to the dangers of cured bacon, not to mention hot fat. Sadly, there seems to be no real substitute for hot bacon fat, but we are not about to give up wilted greens. This recipe will apply to most wild greens, although some should be boiled in 2 waters for the first step, rather than 1.

   1   large handful of amaranth leaves

   1   quart boiling water

   3   tablespoons corn oil

   1   tablespoon lemon juice

   1   tablespoon Wild Herb Vinegar (page 68)

   ½   teaspoon coltsfoot ash

   3   eggs, hard-boiled (optional)

Place amaranth leaves in the bottom of a large kettle. Cover with water and simmer for 20 minutes.

Drain greens well. In a large skillet, heat oil almost to smoking.

Lay greens flat in hot oil for 3–4 minutes. Sprinkle with lemon juice, Wild Herb Vinegar, and coltsfoot ash.

Serve hot with hard-boiled eggs, if desired.

SCALLOPED ARROWHEAD TUBERS

These tiny tubers are vaguely similar to the potato but taste better. Like cooked potatoes, you can use them as a main vegetable and starchy staple. This basic recipe will adapt to most starchy, edible wild tubers and fleshy roots. Let us know what you discover.

- 3 cups arrowhead tubers left whole (*or*, if large, sliced)
- 1 cup wild onions, sliced
- 1 teaspoon peppergrass seeds
- 2 tablespoons parsley, chopped
- ½ teaspoon coltsfoot ash
- 3 tablespoons safflower oil
- 1 cup hot seasoned Wild Vegetable Stock (page 77)

Place arrowhead tubers in a rack over boiling water and steam gently for 20 minutes.

Preheat oven to 400°F.

Place tubers in a glass baking dish. Add onions, peppergrass seeds, 1 tablespoon of the parsley, and the coltsfoot ash. Stir to blend.

Pour oil on top and add Wild Vegetable Stock.

Bake for 45 minutes or until brown and crusty. Sprinkle with remaining parsley and serve as a vegetable with dinner.

BAKED ARROWHEADS

Arrowhead tubers are best stored for a month or more before baking as potatoes.

    1 – 3 arrowhead tubers per person
      1 tablespoon corn oil
      1 tablespoon yogurt
  seasoning to taste

Preheat oven to 400°F.

Wash tubers, wipe dry, and coat well with corn oil.

Place on rack, and bake 20 minutes. Pull out rack and quickly pierce each tuber with a sharp fork. Continue to bake for an additional 20 – 30 minutes.

Split tubers and use fork to flake the starch. Fill with yogurt and season to taste. Serve immediately.

BROILED ARROWHEAD PATTIES

    4 cups arrowhead tubers, cooked and mashed
    ½ cup pine nuts, chopped fine
    6 wild onions, grated
    ¼ cup soy flour

½ teaspoon coltsfoot ash

¾ cup yogurt

2 eggs, beaten

½ cup skim milk

⅛ teaspoon nutmeg

1 cup amaranth seeds (*or* other wild seeds)

Preheat broiler.

In a large bowl, combine all ingredients except seeds. Blend well.

Shape mixture into 8 patties and coat with amaranth seeds. Place on oiled cookie sheet.

Broil patties until lightly browned on both sides.

SAUTÉED DAYLILY WITH ALMONDS

¼ cup safflower oil

2 cups fresh, unopened daylily buds (*or* peeled burdock root)

½ cup sliced almonds (*or* other mild nuts)

Heat oil in a skillet. Add daylily buds all at once. Stir once, then cook over medium heat 3–4 minutes.

Add sliced almonds and stir gently to combine. Remove from heat. Serve hot as a vegetable with dinner.

HERBED DAYLILY BUDS
WITH SUNFLOWER SEEDS

1 cup water

2 cups unopened daylily flower buds

3 tablespoons safflower oil

1 clove garlic, minced

4 wild onions, chopped

1 teaspoon watercress, chopped

½ teaspoon sheepsorrel, chopped

¼ teaspoon basil

⅛ teaspoon thyme

½ teaspoon coltsfoot ash

½ cup sunflower seeds

Bring the water to a fast boil in a saucepan. Drop in daylily buds. Boil 5 minutes. Drain.

Heat safflower oil in a heavy skillet. Add garlic and onions. Sauté until lightly browned.

Add remaining ingredients. Stir to combine and heat briefly.

Add daylily buds and toss lightly to combine. Serve immediately.

day lily

PICKLED SUNCHOKES

- 2 quarts Wild Herb Vinegar (page 68)
- ½ cup honey
- 1 tablespoon sorrel leaves, chopped
- 1 tablespoon fresh dill
- ⅓ cup wild mustard seeds
- 1 tablespoon wild mustard powder
- 1 tablespoon peppergrass seeds
- 3 whole wild ginger roots
- 4 pounds sunchokes (*or* similar starchy roots *or* tubers)

Place Wild Herb Vinegar in a large kettle. Bring to a boil over high heat.

Remove kettle from heat and add all remaining ingredients except sunchokes. Allow to stand until cooled to room temperature.

Wash sunchokes well and slice fairly thin. Place sliced sunchokes in sterilized jars and cover with vinegar mixture. Cover tightly and store 30 days before using.

TUMBLEWEED SHOOTS

Tumbleweed is not so exclusively Western as is commonly supposed. It is widely distributed, perhaps because it loves to travel. Tumbleweed used for food should be very young green shoots no more than 6 inches tall. They should break off easily. They mix well with steamed wild asparagus or other greens.

  1 quart water

  2 cups tumbleweed shoots, cut in pieces

  ¼ cup water

Boil 1 quart water in a large kettle. Add tumbleweed shoots. Return to boil and boil for 10 minutes.

Drain shoots. Rinse under cold running water. In a second kettle, bring ¼ cup water to a full boil under a vegetable rack. Place shoots on rack over boiling water. Steam, covered, about 5 minutes. Drain and serve as is, or combine with other cooked greens.

STEAMED MESQUITE PODS

This is a true wild delicacy that even the most domesticated palate will enjoy. Be sure to use the green pods while they are still fresh. If you have some on hand for quite awhile, dry them well and grind into meal to be used as cornmeal for mush or pancakes.

  10 – 12 fresh green mesquite pods

  ½ teaspoon spicebush

Place mesquite pods on a rack over boiling water. Cover and steam until tender, about 20 minutes.

Sprinkle with spicebush and serve hot with dinner.

COOKED WILD
VEGETABLES
AND GREENS

COOKED MILKWEED

- 2 cups milkweed shoots (*or* flower buds *or* seed pods)
- 1 quart boiling water
- 1 cup boiling water
- 3 tablespoons seasoned oil and vinegar (*or* lemon juice)

Place milkweed in a large kettle. Cover with boiling water. Boil hard for 3 minutes.

Drain and discard first water. Have water boiling in a second kettle or pot. Add drained milkweed. Boil until tender, about 10 minutes.

Drain milkweed and move to serving dish. Sprinkle with seasoned oil and vinegar. Serve hot with dinner.

COOKED DANDELION

Always pick young dandelion plants for cooking *before* the flowers appear.

- 1 large bunch young dandelion plants
- 3 cups boiling water
- ½ cup boiling water
- 2 tablespoons lemon juice

Separate dandelion leaves from roots. Wash roots and

slice thin. Tear off select portions of leaves and discard remainder.

Submerge a rack in a large pot containing 3 cups boiling water. Drop in dandelion roots first, then leaves. Boil for 10 minutes.

Remove rack, draining dandelions. Discard first cooking water. Place dandelion pieces in a vegetable steamer or on a rack over, but not in, the ½ cup water. Cover and steam for 10 minutes. Sprinkle with lemon juice and serve.

COLLECTING AND PRESERVING WILD MUSHROOMS

As we have stressed, this is a cookbook and not a field guide. Before you start to collect wild mushrooms for food, study at least one good field guide. Study it well and carry it with you. Until you become an expert, collect only the wild mushrooms that are easiest to identify. Do not gamble. Death is one of the nicest things that can happen to people who eat the wrong mushroom.

We feel that there is only one satisfactory and safe way to preserve mushrooms. Thread them on a long string, not touching, and hang them to dry in the open air under a hot sun, or dry them by suspending them near the ceiling of your kitchen while you keep the cookstove going. When dry, store in cool, dry, sterile jars and seal tightly. Store jars in a cool, dry place. Use dried mushrooms in sauces and dressings, or restore them by soaking at room temperature for about two hours.

STEAMED WILD MUSHROOMS

Many wild mushrooms are far too large to sauté. Rather than have to slice or chop them, try steaming them.

    3 cups large wild mushrooms
    ¼ cup lemon juice
    ¼ cup safflower oil

Place whole, large mushrooms in a colander. Sprinkle with lemon juice and shake well. Brush with oil, coating well.

Place mushrooms on a rack in a pot above boiling water. Water must not touch mushrooms. Cover and steam until tender, 10–30 minutes. Reserve liquid for soups.

SUNCHOKE CASSEROLE

8	raw sunchokes, cut in pieces
3 or 4	wild onions
1	cup hazelnuts (*or* almonds)
2	eggs
3	tablespoons soy flour
2	tablespoons safflower oil
½	teaspoon coltsfoot ash
½	cup springbeauty tubers
¼	teaspoon thyme
2	tablespoons peppergrass seeds

Preheat oven to 350°F.

Place all but the peppergrass seeds in a blender. Blend well.

Ladle into an oiled casserole dish. Sprinkle with peppergrass seeds. Bake for 1 hour. Serve as main course.

Yield: *4 − 6 servings*

279

PRIMROSE POD STEW

1 pound evening primrose pods

3 tablespoons olive oil

1 cup wild onions, chopped

1 tablespoon sorrel leaves, chopped

1 teaspoon salsify root, minced

2 cups ground cherries, sliced

1 cut section cow parsnip stem base

1 teaspoon peppergrass seeds

½ teaspoon basil

1 tablespoon Ground Cherry Sauce (page 102)

Primrose pods should be held 1 week before using. To prepare for cooking, cover with boiling water, let stand several minutes, then drain. Repeat twice.

Heat olive oil in a large skillet and lightly sauté wild onion. Add sorrel and salsify and cook, stirring constantly, for 5 minutes.

Add ground cherries. Cover and cook 10 minutes.

Add prepared primrose pods and remaining ingredients. Mix thoroughly. Reduce heat and simmer, covered, about 25 minutes. Serve immediately.

Yield: *4 servings*

WILD VEGETABLE LOAF

- 1 cup wild carrots, grated
- 1 cup soybeans, cooked
- 1 cup arrowhead tubers, diced
- ¼ cup wild onions, chopped
- 2 eggs, beaten
- ½ teaspoon watercress, chopped
- ¼ cup rose hips, chopped
- 3 tablespoons cornmeal (*or* acorn meal)
- ½ cup amaranth seeds
- 3 tablespoons Wild Vegetable Stock (page 77)
- ¼ teaspoon coltsfoot ash

Preheat oven to 325°F.

Place all ingredients in a large bowl and blend well.

Mold in an oiled loaf pan and bake for 45−60 minutes. Serve hot or cold.

Yield: *6−8 servings*

WILD ONION, CARROT, AND VENISON PIE

You may leave out the venison for a vegetarian main dish or include it for a hearty meal with very little meat. This is a fine way to use older onions and carrots. Various seeds, tubers, and roots may be used in small amounts.

- 2 cups rye flour (*or* 1½ cups rye flour and ½ cup acorn *or* other wild meal)
- 1 teaspoon coltsfoot ash
- ¼ cup safflower oil
- 2 tablespoons small wild seeds

ice water to blend pastry

- ¾ cup wild carrots, sliced and steamed
- 1½ cups wild onions, sliced and steamed
- ¾ cup dried or jerked venison (*or* other game), cubed
- 1 cup cheddar cheese, grated
- 2 tablespoons olive oil
- 1 cup soy milk
- 3 eggs, beaten
- ¼ teaspoon wild spicebush (*or* allspice *or* thyme)

In a bowl, combine flour, ½ teaspoon of the coltsfoot ash, oil, and seeds. Blend while adding enough water to make a stiff dough. Line 2 oiled pie pans and chill.

Preheat oven to 350°F.

Combine carrots, onions, and venison. Divide equally into pie shells. Sprinkle with grated cheese.

Combine oil, milk, eggs, seasoning, and ½ teaspoon coltsfoot ash. Blend and pour over cheese.

Bake for 30 minutes. Serve 1 pie as a main course with wild soup, acorn muffins, and herb tea. Refrigerate the other pie and slice cold for breakfast or lunch.

Yield: *6 – 8 servings*

YAMPA CASSEROLE

2 cups yampa roots, steamed and peeled

1 cup rye bread crumbs

2 eggs, slightly beaten

½ cup soy milk

1 teaspoon coltsfoot ash

¼ cup corn oil

½ cup granola

Preheat oven to 350°F.

Grate or dice the yampa roots. Place in a mixing bowl and add all ingredients except granola. Mix thoroughly.

Place mixture in an oiled casserole dish and sprinkle with granola. Bake for 45 minutes and serve hot.

Yield: *4 servings*

WILD MUSHROOM CASSEROLE

We usually prefer to sauté mushrooms in oil, but a surplus can be made up into this casserole.

 3 cups wild mushrooms, sliced

 ¼ cup lemon juice

 ¼ cup safflower oil

 ½ cup wild onions, chopped

 ½ teaspoon coltsfoot ash

 1 teaspoon marjoram

 ½ teaspoon rosemary

 ¼ teaspoon thyme

 ½ cup hot Dark Game Stock (page 72) (*or* Wild Fowl Stock [page 74] *or* Wild Vegetable Stock [page 77])

Preheat oven to 325°F.

Sprinkle sliced mushrooms with lemon juice.

Heat oil in a heavy skillet. Sauté wild onions very lightly.

Add wild mushrooms by the cupful, sauté lightly, and move aside to allow for the next cupful.

Add coltsfoot ash and herbs. Combine well.

Move herbed mushrooms into an oiled casserole dish. Pour on hot stock. Bake, covered, for 30 minutes. Serve hot. May be refrigerated and reheated once.

Yield: *4 –6 servings*

WILD VEGETABLE STEW

This is a vegetarian stew, but the recipe is flexible. You could add small amounts of cooked, cubed game meat to it and almost any wild edible, including roots, tubers, seeds, stems, and greens.

    2 tablespoons corn oil
    1 cup wild onions, chopped
    ½ cup wild carrots, chopped
    ½ cup wild nettle (*or* Indian potato), cut in pieces
    ¼ cup wild parsnip, chopped
    ¼ cup springbeauty (*or* sweet clover root), chopped
    1 cup ground cherries, slightly mashed
    ½ teaspoon dill
    ½ teaspoon tarragon
    ½ teaspoon coltsfoot ash (*or* lemon juice)
    2 cups hot Wild Vegetable Stock (page 77)

Heat oil in a large kettle or stew pot. Add wild onions and sauté lightly.

Add remaining ingredients and cover with Wild Vegetable Stock. Simmer, covered, for 2 hours. Add more hot stock if necessary. Serve with biscuits.

Yield: *6 servings*

MUSTARD CUSTARD DINNER

Mustard greens are widely prized, and well they should be. Although there is considerable quality and taste variation among the several species, all are edible and all are nutritious. Most people love these wild greens simply steamed and served in moderation with organ meats. Here is a somewhat more elaborate recipe.

1 pound wild mustard greens

¾ cup water

3 tablespoons safflower oil

½ cup wild onions, chopped

4 tablespoons rye flour

1 teaspoon coltsfoot ash

½ teaspoon tarragon

2 cups yogurt

4 egg yolks, beaten smooth

4 egg whites, beaten stiff

1 recipe Steamed Wild Rice (page 298)

1 tablespoon wild caraway seeds

Wash greens well under cold running water. Remove tough stems and ribs. Place the leaves and tender stems in a saucepan. Add water, bring to a boil, reduce heat, and simmer, covered, for 20 minutes. Drain and chop.

Heat oil in a large, heavy saucepan. Add wild onions and sauté. Stir in flour, coltsfoot ash, and tarragon and blend well.

Stir in yogurt gradually. Do not allow to boil. Reduce heat to very low and cook while stirring constantly for 3 or 4 minutes.

Remove saucepan from heat and stir in beaten egg yolks. Return to low heat and cook while stirring until mixture thickens. Stir in cooked wild mustard greens. Remove from heat and allow to cool for 20 minutes at room temperature.

Preheat oven to 350°F.

Gently fold in beaten egg whites. Pour mixture into an oiled ring mold. Set mold in a shallow pan of hot water and bake for 45 minutes.

Turn the set custard onto a heated serving dish. Fill center with Steamed Wild Rice and sprinkle with caraway seeds.

Yield: *4 −6 servings*

MILKWEED PODS AND WILD RICE

- 3 cups fresh, green, immature milkweed pods
- 1 recipe Steamed Wild Rice (page 298)
- 1 teaspoon Wild Herb Vinegar (page 68)
- ¼ teaspoon basil
- ⅛ teaspoon rosemary
- ⅛ teaspoon thyme
- ⅛ teaspoon sage

Place milkweed pods in a kettle and cover with boiling water. Place over moderate heat and boil steadily for 3 minutes. Drain.

Again cover pods with boiling water. Boil 5 minutes and drain.

Place pods on a rack in a vegetable steamer over boiling water. Add Wild Herb Vinegar to the water. Cover tightly and steam until very tender, about 20 minutes.

Place Steamed Wild Rice in a mound in the center of a large serving platter. Arrange hot steamed milkweed pods around sides.

Combine herbs and sprinkle on top. Serve at once.

Yield: *4 servings*

WILD ASPARAGUS
AND CHICKWEED PIE

½ pound wild asparagus, cut and steamed

½ pound fresh, young chickweed stems

½ cup parsley, chopped

1 cup wild onions, chopped

⅛ teaspoon coltsfoot ash

½ teaspoon rosemary

⅛ teaspoon spicebush

2 tablespoons safflower oil

½ cup cheddar cheese, grated

pastry for 1 pie crust

Preheat oven to 425°F.

Combine all ingredients except cheese and blend well. Place in a kettle and slowly heat, mixing occasionally, for about 7 minutes.

Place in an oiled casserole dish and cover with pie crust. Sprinkle crust with grated cheddar cheese. Bake for 20 minutes. Serve hot as main course.

Yield: *4 servings*

CHAPTER TWELVE

WILD GRAINS, BREADS, AND CEREALS

A great many edible wild plants have parts which may be processed or dried and then ground into flour or meal. The best-known sources of forager flour are acorns, cattails, and grain grasses, but other plants are important to local foragers. The following is a comprehensive list of such selected plants.

Making flour or meal is rather simple but often time-consuming and laborious. The process usually involves a careful cleaning and drying, peeling, roasting, or boiling (in the case of rootstocks), and grinding or milling. Experimentation will suggest uses; in general, any wild flour or meal may be used in any recipe.

Acorn

See white oak.

Amaranth. *Amaranthus* spp.

Amaranth seeds appear in abundance in late summer or early fall. Gather them by pulling the plants, drying them in sacks, then shaking to release the seeds. Sift, winnow, and grind the seeds into meal.

Arrowgrass. *Triglochin maritima*

Arrowgrass seeds may be gathered and ground into a flour similar to wheat. This is true of most grasses, and of all jointed-stem grasses in particular. A real danger in using any grass or similar plant is the fungus, ergot. Ergot may infect any of the cereal plants, forming black sclerotia or branching masses of black filaments which replace many of the seeds of the host plant. Visually, the fungus resembles a rooster's spur and from this resemblence gains the name "cock's spur." It is an extremely dangerous poison for humans, although it is also a source of several beneficial medicines. The safest course is to avoid any cereal plant that displays black seeds or scales.

Biscuitroot. *Lomatium* spp.

After digging, dry the roots for a few days, then peel. Dry the core thoroughly before grinding into flour.

Blue verbena. *Verbena hastata*

Seeds may be lightly roasted, ground into a meal, and

then leached in the same manner as acorn meal.

Broad-leaf plantain (Indian wheat, plantain).
Plantago major

Grind the seeds into meal.

Bulrush (tule). *Scirpus* spp.

Here again bulrush proves to be a very useful plant. Roots, pollen, and seeds will all produce a flour or meal. Roots for this purpose may be gathered at any time of the year. Young, tender roots need only be dried thoroughly and ground into a fine flour. Older roots need to be sieved to separate scales and pieces. When the flowers are in bloom, the pollen is easy to shake into sacks. Like cattail pollen, you can then press it into cakes or combine it with other flours for any baking purpose. When the bulrush goes into seed, thrash the seeds off the plants into baskets and then grind them into meal. Or use them whole by combining them with acorn, corn, or similar meals. All parts of bulrush are nutritious.

Canary grass. *Phalaris canariensis*

This is the same plant that produces the seeds used in birdseed. It is a long-grained grass, very nutritious and flavorful. The grain, like all others, must be checked and cleaned very carefully to avoid the danger of mold, bugs, or ergot poisoning. After this process, the grain may be cooked as a cereal, combined with other grains, or milled into a delightful and useful flour or meal.

Cattail. *Typha* spp.

Use both the pollen and the roots of all cattails to make flour or meal. Roots of any age may be ground into flour. Peel them first, then dry thoroughly, and sift the flour. When the flower spikes are bright yellow and very ripe but still firm, shake the pollen and the small flowers from the spikes into sacks. The flour is very high in protein and, when mixed with more ordinary flours, has an enriching effect. It is as delicious as it is nutritious and a tablespoon or two will replace the same quantity of flour in any pancake, muffin, or biscuit recipe with miraculous results.

Goosefoot. *Chenopodium Fremontii*

Goosefoot has very small seeds that may be used raw and are excellent when combined with acorn, cattail, or cornmeal. These combinations can produce some delicious cereals and cakes.

Hazelnut (filbert). *Corylus cornuta* and *C. americana*

Either species of hazelnut makes an excellent meal when ground as finely as possible. Combine it with flour in recipes for cakes, pancakes, and breads.

Juniper berries. *Juniperus* spp.

Each of the *Juniperus* species produces fruit that is legendary among foragers and gourmets all over the world. The fruits resemble small, hard berries, usually blue or blue green. They are locally plentiful, even in winter. Though high in natural sugars they're not very good to eat raw, and are often used as a seasoning or flavoring. The berries may be ground into an excellent meal to add to cereals and cakes. Use the meal to dust fish or fowl pieces for baking or frying.

Knotweed. *Polygonum* spp.

Press knotweed seeds into cakes or grind into flour.

Mountain rice (ricegrass). *Oryzopsis* spp.

The seeds of any of this group of grasses are good for grinding into meal or flour.

Pond lily (waterlily). *Nuphar polysepalum*

Dig the large roots or tubers in early fall. Peel them, slice the core, and then dry thoroughly. When dry, grind the sliced roots into a meal; leach the meal in the same way as for acorn meal (see page 299).

Reed grass (carrizo). *Phragmites communis*

Use reed grass seeds whole, as a grain cereal, or grind them into nutritious all-purpose flour.

Sage. *Salvia columbariae*

Seeds may be ground into an unusual flour. A little sage flour, combined with wild oat flour, makes a great crust for venison and small-game pies.

Serviceberry. *Amelanchier* spp.

Dry serviceberries thoroughly, then grind into a very coarse meal. Use the dried berries in cakes and stew dumplings.

Shepherd's purse. *Capsella bursa-pastoris*

Seeds may be ground into flour.

Sugar grass (manna grass). *Glyceria* spp.

All species produce abundant seeds which may be ground into an excellent flour.

Sunflower. *Helianthus* spp.

Most sunflowers produce quantities of large seeds and any local variety is worth grinding into meal. The meal is best when mixed with cornmeal or acorn meal, but it may also be used alone.

Water shield. *Brosenia schreberi*

Water shield produces thick roots that may be dried, then ground into a starchy flour. In recipes, it behaves much as potato or rice flour.

White oak. *Quercus* spp.

White oak acorns make the best meal. For many, acorn meal is the most important of all foods from the wild. It is used in countless wilderness recipes and throughout this book. Details of the procedure for processing acorns into meal appear on page 299.

Wild cabbage (squaw cabbage). *Caulanthus crassicaulis*

Seeds may be ground into flour.

Wild caraway (swamproot, yampa).

Perideridia spp.

This versatile and flavorful wild root has several uses, not the least of which is as a nutritious and delicious flour. Roots must first be thoroughly dried, then stone ground as finely as possible.

Wild rye and wild oat. *Elymus* spp. and

Avena spp.

Sometime in the early sixties, Parp was befriended by a self-sufficient family somewhere in central Oregon. These wonderful folks lived far from any road, about seven horseback miles into the wilds. Their beautiful home was fully equipped for self-sufficiency, complete with an old stone hand mill. They each took weekly turns at this mill, easily producing all of their own flour. One of their choicest products was wild rye flour, which they ground quite fine and used for most of their baking needs. The grinding was, of course, the last step in the long and tedious task of harvesting the grain of wild rye, checking it for parasites or mold, thrashing and cleaning, and, finally, performing the painstaking task of singeing the hair from the grain before grinding or cooking. This same process applies to wild oat. The best variety of wild rye is *Elymus triticoides* and the best oat is *Avena fatua.* Both are quite widespread in North America.

STEAMED WILD RICE

Wild rice is economical only if you gather your own. This takes time and effort but is well worth it considering the price one must pay in the market. Be sure to dry it thoroughly, then parch in a hot oven to loosen the husks. Wild rice will store indefinitely but must be washed well in cold running water before cooking. Steamed wild rice is a wild foods staple and we have included it in many recipes. In general, one may substitute cooked brown or white rice, if necessary.

- 3 cups boiling water
- ½ teaspoon coltsfoot ash (*or* lemon juice)
- 1 cup wild rice, washed

Combine water and coltsfoot ash and bring to a full boil over high heat.

Slowly add wild rice so boiling does not stop. Stir once, gently. Reduce heat and simmer, uncovered, 30–40 minutes or until tender.

Preheat oven to 300°F.

Drain rice, if necessary, and place in a baking dish. Set baking dish in a shallow pan of boiling water and bake for 20 minutes. Serve plain or seasoned, alone or as a side dish. Sautéed onions are excellent with this.

Yield: *4 servings*

ACORN MEAL

- 2 pounds sun-dried white oak acorns (*or* other acorns)
- 1 small cheesecloth bag
- 1 larger canvas bag
- 1 source constantly running cold water (creek or faucet)

Use a fine stone mill to grind the acorns into a fine meal. Sift to remove sharp pieces.

Place the meal in a cheesecloth bag and place that in a canvas bag.

Suspend the bags below the faucet or immerse the bags, tied securely, in a fast-running, clean water stream. Allow 3 days of this to remove most of the tannin. Knead the meal thoroughly at least 3 times each day.

Remove leached meal from bags and place the mass on a stainless steel sheet to dry in the sun. As the meal dries, separate the dried flour from the outside of the mass. When it is all dried, run the meal through the mill again to restore to flour. Mix half-and-half, or less, with other flour in any recipe.

WILD
GRAINS,
BREADS, AND
CEREALS

PARP'S PURE ACORN BREAD OR CAKES

If one spends a long period in the woods, especially in the dense forests of the Midwest and East, this recipe will provide an adequate substitute for bread. It helps to harvest a little wild honey to overcome the rather flat flavor.

    2   cups acorn meal, leached
    ½   teaspoon coltsfoot ash
    1   cup cold water

Campfire to glowing coals.

Place acorn flour in a bowl or pot. Add coltsfoot ash and mix thoroughly.

Gradually pour in water while stirring with a fork. Knead with fingers to produce a stiff dough.

Spread the dough evenly in the bottom of a pot and cover tightly. Place pot above glowing coals and bake 30 minutes, or use the following method:

Heat a small amount of corn oil in a heavy skillet over medium-high heat. Form dough into cakes about 3 inches in diameter and ¾ inch thick. Place cakes in hot oil. Turn to brown both sides, then move the skillet further from the heat and bake until done. Serve with wild fruit, berries, or honey.

ACORN-RYE MUFFINS

¾ cup rye flour

¾ cup acorn meal

¼ cup soy flour

1 teaspoon baking powder

½ teaspoon baking soda

1 cup yogurt

2 tablespoons light honey

1 egg, beaten light

Preheat oven to 400°F.

Sift all dry ingredients together twice and place in a large mixing bowl.

Combine yogurt, honey, and egg, and stir to mix thoroughly.

Quickly add yogurt mixture to dry mixture. Stir very lightly, no more than 20−25 strokes. Dough should be lumpy.

Place dough in well-greased muffin tins to about ⅔ full. Immediately place in oven for 30 minutes. Let stand 5 minutes before serving muffins from tins. Serve with honey.

Yield: *12 muffins*

ACORN SPOON BREAD

The consistency of acorn flour is especially suited to this traditional treat, which makes a fine, hot accompaniment to fresh trout, bear ham, or roast wildfowl.

      ½ cup acorn meal
      ½ cup cornmeal
      1 teaspoon baking powder
      1 egg, beaten
      1 tablespoon dark honey
   1½ cups soy milk
      1 tablespoon corn oil

Preheat oven to 375°F.

Combine and sift together all dry ingredients.

Gradually stir in egg, honey, and 1 cup of the soy milk.

Use the oil to brush the inside of a medium-size glass baking dish. Pour in the batter, make a cavity, and fill with the remaining ½ cup soy milk.

Bake for 50 minutes or until quite crusty. Serve hot with warm honey.

Yield: *6 servings*

ACORN MUSH

Acorn mush is a versatile food that can be served hot with Wild Fruit or Berry Sauce (page 338), baked as a breakfast cake, or combined with other foods. Be sure your acorn meal is leached, dried, and reground to a fine meal.

  1 cup acorn meal (*or* ½ cup acorn meal and ½ cup cornmeal)

  1 cup cold Dark Game Stock (page 72)

  2 cups hot Dark Game Stock

  4 tablespoons yeast

  1 teaspoon lemon juice

In a large mixing bowl, combine meal and cold stock. Stir with wire whisk to mix thoroughly.

Stir in hot stock, yeast, and lemon juice. Pour mixture into a double boiler over hot water and cook for 40 minutes.

Serve mush as a hot cereal, or pour into a loaf pan and chill 12 hours before using for other purposes.

Yield: *4 servings*

SOURDOUGH ACORN BREAD

1	cup cornmeal
½	cup acorn meal
1¾	cups milk
2	eggs
2	tablespoons dark honey
1	cup sourdough starter
¼	cup corn oil
¾	teaspoon baking soda

Preheat oven to 425°F.

Combine cornmeal and acorn meal in a large bowl. Add milk, eggs, honey, and starter. Beat well.

Add oil and baking soda. Stir until well blended.

Ladle into a Dutch oven or heavy skillet and bake for 30 – 35 minutes. Serve hot.

FRUIT AND NUT BREAD

⅓	cup warm water
3	tablespoons honey

2	teaspoons yeast
1¾	cups boiling water
2	tablespoons oil
1	cup wild rice flour
1	cup oat flour
1½	cups rye flour
½	teaspoon cloves
½	cup wild fruit (*or* berries)
¼	cup nuts, crushed

Combine warm water and honey. Add yeast to dissolve.

In a large mixing bowl, combine boiling water and oil. Combine flours and add to hot water mixture. Allow to cool somewhat.

Add yeast mixture and beat for 3 minutes. Cover with a damp cloth and set in a pan of hot water to rise for 2 hours. Beat for another 3 minutes. Fold in cloves, fruit, and nuts.

Move the dough to an oiled loaf pan and set in a warm, dark place to rise for 45 minutes.

Preheat oven to 400°F.

Place loaf in the oven and immediately reduce the heat to 325°F. Bake for 45 minutes and cool before serving.

EGGS POACHED IN ACORN MUSH

1   loaf Acorn Mush (page 303), chilled 12 hours

3   tablespoons corn oil

6   eggs

1   tablespoon cold water

1   teaspoon coltsfoot ash

Slice cold Acorn Mush into 6 pieces.

In a large skillet, heat oil but do not allow to smoke. Sauté sliced mush until brown on both sides.

Remove skillet from heat and use a tablespoon to form a cavity in each piece of mush. Break 1 egg into each cavity.

Place skillet over medium-low heat and add the cold water to the center of the pan. Cover tightly and cook until eggs are done to taste. Sprinkle with coltsfoot ash and serve immediately.

Yield: 3 – 6 servings

skillet

PARP'S DUMPLINGS

    1 cup rye flour

    1 cup wild rice flour

    ½ cup acorn meal

    1 tablespoon baking powder

    ½ teaspoon coltsfoot ash

    1 cup soy milk

    1 tablespoon safflower oil

Sift flours, acorn meal, baking powder, and coltsfoot ash together into a large bowl.

In a small bowl, combine soy milk and safflower oil.

Add milk mixture to flour mixture, blending slowly and thoroughly.

Knead dough lightly on a flour-dusted board.

Gently shape dumplings into balls the size of 1 teaspoonful each.

Drop balls into hot stew. Cook 15 minutes, uncovered. Serve immediately.

PARPCAKES WITH WILD FRUIT, NUTS, OR BERRIES

This recipe makes Parp's favorite pancake breakfast. The granola and all of the spices are optional and any berry or fruit may be used.

1 egg

1 cup buttermilk

2 tablespoons oil

¾ cup whole wheat flour

1 tablespoon honey

1 teaspoon baking powder

½ teaspoon baking soda

¼ teaspoon cinnamon

⅛ teaspoon nutmeg

⅛ teaspoon ginger

¼ cup granola

½ cup any wild fruit (*or* berries *or* ¼ cup crushed nuts)

Preheat griddle to 375°F.

Crack egg into a large mixing bowl and beat lightly with a fork.

Add buttermilk, oil, flour, honey, baking powder, soda, spices, granola, and fruit (if desired) in that order. Beat until fairly smooth.

Pour batter by ¼ cupfuls on hot, greased griddle. When the edges dry slightly and pancakes puff, turn once. Bake other side until golden brown. Serve topped with Wild Fruit Sauce (page 338) or honey.

Yield: *8 – 10 pancakes*

GOOSEFOOT MUFFINS

- ¼ cup goosefoot (*or* similar) seeds
- ½ teaspoon coltsfoot ash
- ¾ cup wild meal (acorn, crabgrass, *or* juniper berry)
- 1 cup oat flour
- 4 teaspoons baking powder
- 1 cup milk
- 1 egg
- 1 tablespoon warm honey
- ¼ cup corn oil

Preheat oven to 425°F.

Place goosefoot seeds in a large mixing bowl. Sprinkle with coltsfoot ash and toss to combine.

Add wild meal, oat flour, and baking powder. Blend well.

Add remaining ingredients. Beat briskly until as smooth as possible.

Pour batter into well-oiled muffin cups. Bake for 20 minutes. Serve hot, with honey.

Yield: *12 muffins*

STEAMED CATTAIL BREAD

- 2 tablespoons yeast
- ¼ cup lukewarm water
- ½ cup cattail pollen flour
- ½ cup acorn meal
- ⅓ cup skim milk powder
- ¾ cup currants, soaked overnight
- ¾ cup yogurt
- ½ cup molasses
- ½ cup cracked canary grass grain (*or* wheat germ *or* cornmeal)

Place yeast in water. Place all dry ingredients in a large mixing bowl and mix to combine well. Add currants and stir.

Combine soaked yeast with yogurt and molasses. Add to dry ingredients. Stir in cracked canary grass.

Pour dough into two well-oiled baking tins of about 1-pint capacity. Cover with brown sacks tied with strings.

Place baking tins on a rack in a steamer. Add boiling water to fill halfway up the sides of the tins. Cover tightly and steam for 2 hours.

JUNIPER BERRY BREAD

1   cup juniper berry meal (*or* ½ cup juniper berry
    meal and ½ cup corn, acorn, crabgrass, *or*
    similar meal, *or* rye flour)

1   cup oat flour

4   teaspoons baking powder

1   cup milk

1   egg

1   tablespoon warm honey

¼   cup corn oil

Preheat oven to 425°F.

Combine juniper berry meal with oat flour and baking
powder in a mixing bowl. Blend well.

Add milk, egg, honey, and corn oil. Beat briskly until
quite smooth.

Place mixture in an oiled 8-inch-square baking pan.
Bake for about 25 minutes. Serve hot with honey or
Wild Berry Sauce (page 338).

CRABGRASS CEREAL

Crabgrass seeds are plentiful nearly everywhere and may be ground or run through a food processor to create a very coarse meal.

3 cups water
1 cup crabgrass seeds, coarsely ground (*or* other wild cereal)

Place water in a pot over high heat. Bring to a full rolling boil.

Stir in crabgrass meal slowly to keep water boiling. Stir and boil for 30 seconds.

Cover pot tightly and reduce heat. Cook 15 minutes.

Remove pot from heat and leave covered. Let stand 5 minutes. Serve with berry topping and soy milk, or honey and coconut milk.

Yield: *4 servings*

CHAPTER THIRTEEN

WILD FRUIT AND NUTS

Parp observes that, in spite of Muskrat's dreams, there is no land where pork loin sandwiches drop from the trees. This by way of saying the obvious: there is nothing as good as the food that appears ready to eat—naturally—on bushes, trees, and plants in all seasons and almost all climates. Parp also says we often carry this cooking thing too far—there is no improving on a handful of fresh filberts or a "wild" apple. You may choose to serve chilled yogurt with any fresh, wild fruit, but combining nature's gifts with alcohol must surely be a sin.

Most of the recipes in this chapter call for fruits that are not usually eaten straight from the bush but are excellent ingredients for sauces, jams, souffles, and preserves. Other fruits are best eaten plain and fresh, or frozen and served later with yogurt or grain cereals. Some of our recipes, like Wild Berry Fritters and Curried Wild Fruit, are designed to make good use of canned, frozen, overripe, or damaged fruit.

All of this generally holds for nuts, as well. Fresh piñon nuts really are improved by roasting, and chestnuts are only edible in stews or roasted. We do not include recipes for candied almonds and the like.

 WILD
FRUIT AND
NUTS

BERRIES

Raspberries, blackberries, thimbleberries, dewberries, and blackcaps are closely related. All are from the Rose family and may be eaten raw or used in jams, jellies, or pies. They are less acceptable in breads or pancakes. They are extremely common all over North America. Be sure of your identification when dealing with the less common, less obvious species, especially the lighter colored berries. Consult authoritative field guides regarding these plants, except for the unmistakable raspberries and blackberries.

Serviceberries and mountain ash berries may be eaten raw, cooked, or sun-dried. When ripe, the berries are sweet, especially if they've gone through an early frost. Bitter, unripe berries should be avoided. The mountain ash is native to most of North America and is quite common and easy to identify. Serviceberries come earlier in the season than mountain ash berries and the two together cover a full six months of the year, from mid-spring through early autumn. Use both serviceberries and mountain ash berries in any berry pie recipe, and in pancakes, muffins, and breads. Both make excellent jams and jellies.

DRYING WILD FRUITS

Most edible wild fruits may be dried and stored for future use. In the arid Southwest, sun-drying is the most practical method, but other climates require other methods. The most important thing is to dry your fruits as quickly as possible in order to lessen the loss of vitamins that pass off with the water. Bruised, overripe, or blemished fruit will not dry properly and will often ruin an entire batch of dried fruit.

We believe that no ingredients should be added to fruit before it is dried. Naturally dried fruit will lose some of its color and may turn brown if cut or sliced, but the taste will be superb.

Large fruit should be pared, cored, and sliced before drying. Smaller fruit should be stemmed and pitted as necessary. Spread your fruit one layer deep with plenty of air space all around. Use flat drying trays with screen bottoms for circulation. The top of the tray should also be covered with screen or cheesecloth arranged so as not to touch the tops of the fruit. The trays should be turned often to allow full drying. If you can sun-dry outdoors, simply set your trays on rocks or timbers well aboveground in an area of circulating air. If you must dry indoors, place your trays (constructed of nonflammable materials) in a very slow oven.

Please note that properly dried fruits are not completely dried all the way through but will retain moist flesh inside. The outside of the fruit should be dry and leathery. Fruit will usually sun-dry in one arid day or about six hours in a 175°F oven.

WILD
FRUIT AND
NUTS

GROUND CHERRY JAM

   5 cups ground cherries, crushed

   1 lemon

   3 tablespoons water

   1 2½-ounce package dried fruit pectin

   7 cups light honey

Husk, wash, and crush enough ground cherries to produce 5 cups. Place in a deep kettle.

Squeeze the juice of the lemon into the ground cherries. Grate the lemon peel and add this also. Add water and pectin and mix well.

Place over high heat and bring to a full boil, stirring constantly. Pour in honey while stirring vigorously.

Again, bring the mixture to a full boil. Boil hard for 2 minutes, stirring constantly. Remove from heat.

Allow mixture to settle and cool slightly. Skim surface. Scoop into prepared jars, cover with paraffin, and seal.

GROUND CHERRY PRESERVES

  1½ cups honey

   1 cup water

  ½ lemon, sliced

  ½ teaspoon ground cinnamon

   4 cups ground cherries, washed

Combine honey and water in a saucepan. Add lemon slices and cinnamon. Bring close to a boil over medium heat.

Add ground cherries and bring to a gentle boil. Simmer for about 1 hour. Pour into sterile jars and seal.

GROUND CHERRY SOUFFLÉ

This recipe makes a main course of ground cherries.

- 2 cups ground cherries, mashed
- 3 tablespoons safflower oil
- ½ teaspoon lemon juice
- ½ teaspoon tarragon
- 3 tablespoons rye flour
- ½ teaspoon spicebush
- ½ teaspoon dill
- 4 egg yolks, beaten smooth
- 4 egg whites, beaten until stiff

Preheat oven to 350°F.

In a large mixing bowl, combine all ingredients except egg whites.

Gently fold egg whites into mixture. Do not stir.

Pour mixture into oiled casserole. Bake for 40 minutes. Serve with Acorn-Rye Muffins (page 301) and cold herb tea.

GOOSEBERRY PUDDING

All gooseberries and currants are edible raw or cooked. The best and most common approach is to sun-dry the berries and then use them in breads or as trail snacks or in pemmican. Undried, use them for pies, preserves, and various desserts and sauces. Gooseberries and currants may be frozen dry or in a light honey syrup.

    2 cups sun-dried gooseberries

    3 cups milk, scalded

 1½ cups cold milk

    1 cup cornmeal

  ¼ cup molasses

    1 teaspoon lemon juice

  ½ cup dark honey

  ½ teaspoon ginger

  ¼ teaspoon nutmeg

Combine gooseberries with scalded milk in a saucepan. Place over very low heat.

Combine 1 cup of the cold milk with the cornmeal. Gradually stir this into the gooseberry/hot milk mixture while stirring constantly. Heat and stir until mixture thickens, about 10 minutes.

Preheat oven to 300°F.

Add molasses, lemon juice, honey, ginger, and nutmeg. Pour into a large casserole dish. Pour remaining cold milk onto the middle of the pudding.

Place casserole dish in a large pan. Pour cold water into the pan so that it rises about 2 inches up around the casserole.

Place pan and casserole in oven and bake for 3 hours. After baking, remove the casserole from the pan and allow to cool at room temperature overnight. Serve chilled.

GOOSEBERRY PRESERVES

    4 cups fresh gooseberries
    ¼ cup plus 2 tablespoons water
    3 cups light honey

Place gooseberries in a saucepan. Add water and place over high heat. Bring to a full boil.

With berries boiling briskly, gradually stir in the honey. Lower heat and simmer 25 minutes. Pour into prepared jars and seal. Serve with eggs, meat, or savory vegetable dishes.

CURRANT JELLY

    2 quarts currants

    ½ cup water

    4 cups light honey

Select and wash currants carefully but do not remove stems. Place about ½ cup of currants in the bottom of a pot and mash to extract some juice. Add and mash remaining currants, 1 cup at a time. Add water.

Place over moderate heat and bring to a boil. Simmer until the currants lose their color.

Drain the juice through a jelly bag and measure. Add ¾ cup honey for each cup of juice.

Place mixture over moderate heat and boil until it jells. Pour into prepared jars and cover with paraffin.

RAW BERRY JAM

This is the best way to prepare a jam of raspberries, blackberries, or similar berries.

    2 cups very ripe berries (raspberries,
       blackberries, thimbleberries, dewberries, *or*
       blackcaps)

    1 cup light honey

    ½ teaspoon lemon juice

Wash berries, which need not be carefully selected. Place in a chilled bowl.

Add honey and lemon juice. Crush berries and mix well. Store covered in the refrigerator up to 2 months.

BUNCHBERRY PUDDING

This is another berry that is widespread in North America. It also may be eaten raw or cooked, in jams or in breads.

- 2 cups bunchberries
- 1½ cups hot water
- ¼ cup dark honey
- ¼ teaspoon ginger
- ⅓ cup cornstarch
- ¼ cup cold water
- 1 tablespoon lemon juice
- 2 egg whites

In a large saucepan, gently combine berries, hot water, honey, and ginger.

Dissolve cornstarch in cold water and gently stir into berry mixture. Place over medium heat and cook, stirring gently from the bottom, until it thickens.

Add lemon juice. Beat egg whites stiff. Fold gently into the pudding. Chill and scoop into individual dishes.

WILD BERRY FRITTERS

Use any wild berry that you have frozen or canned in syrup.

- 3 cups corn (*or* safflower) oil
- 4 cups rye (*or* oat) flour
- 3 teaspoons baking powder
- 5 eggs
- ½ cup syrup from the berries
- ½ cup honey
- 3 cups berries, frozen (*or* canned), thawed and drained well

Place oil in a deep kettle over medium-low heat. Allow to heat gradually, to avoid burning or smoking, while preparing remaining ingredients.

Sift dry ingredients together. In a separate bowl, combine eggs, berry syrup, and honey. Beat until frothy.

Quickly mix egg mixture into dry ingredients. Do not beat. Gently fold in berries.

When oil reaches 350°F, drop berry/batter mixture in by tablespoons. Do not crowd. Turn fritters frequently until well done all over. Drain and serve hot.

WILD FRUIT CASSEROLE

The dried huckleberries in this recipe are an excellent substitute for raisins. They also make good trail food.

- ½ cup currants (*or* dried huckleberries)
- ½ cup wild strawberries
- 2 cups wild rice, steamed
- 2 cups wild nuts, chopped
- ⅓ cup safflower oil
- ½ teaspoon coltsfoot ash (*or* lemon juice)
- 1 tablespoon dark honey

Soak currants overnight in water at room temperature.

Preheat oven to 350°F.

Place currants and strawberries in a colander and rinse under cold running water. Drain and mix well.

Combine currants, strawberries, rice, and nuts in an oiled casserole dish.

Stir in oil, coltsfoot ash, and honey. Bake for 40 minutes. Serve as main dish.

Yield: *6 servings*

ROSE HIP OR CHOKECHERRY STEW

A fine and nourishing hot stew may be made from the fruit of either the wild rose or the common chokecherry shrub. The stew is very nutritious and particularly high in natural vitamin C.

3 cups rose hips (*or* chokecherries), cleaned and washed

3 cups water

3 tablespoons fresh lemon juice

1 whole lemon peel, grated

¼ teaspoon allspice (*or* spicebush)

2 sunchokes, cut in small pieces

1 teaspoon dark honey

Combine all ingredients in a stew pot or Crock-Pot. Bring to full boil for 5 minutes.

Reduce heat and simmer, uncovered, for 2 hours. Serve hot in bowls with salad and bread.

Yield: *6 servings*

BERRIES IN BERRY SAUCE

This is an attractive and refreshing dessert for hot afternoons or when cooking away from your kitchen.

¼ cup light honey
1 tablespoon warm water
4 cups fresh wild berries, chilled

In a melting pot, combine the honey and the water. Place over very low heat and stir to blend. You only want to thin the honey, not cook it.

Separate 1 cup of the berries and leave the rest to continue chilling. Press the 1 cup through a sieve to create a very juicy pulp. Combine the pulp with the thin honey mixture and stir. Chill for 1 hour.

When ready to serve, place whole, chilled berries in chilled individual serving dishes and top with sauce.

rose-hips

CURRIED WILD FRUIT

This recipe will accommodate any combination of wild fruits and berries.

- 2 quarts mixed wild fruits and berries
- 1 cup Wildfowl Stock (page 74)
- 1 cup wild fruit juice
- 1 tablespoon curry powder
- 1 tablespoon tapioca
- 3 tablespoons cold water
- 1 cup sliced nuts
- ½ cup currants
- 1 cup coconut, grated (optional)

Clean and cut fruit so that pieces are all about the same size as the smallest berries.

Combine Wildfowl Stock, fruit juice, and curry powder in a saucepan over medium heat. Bring to a simmer and cook for ½ hour.

Combine tapioca and water in a small, lidded jar. Cover and shake to blend well. Pour the mixture into the hot sauce while stirring constantly. Continue to cook and stir until mixture thickens.

Add fruit, nuts, currants, and coconut. Serve with baked fish or fowl.

Yield: *6 servings*

WILD FRUIT OR BERRY JUICE CUSTARDS

- 1 cup sweet, fresh wild fruit (*or* berry) juice, warmed
- ½ cup light honey
- 4 egg yolks, well beaten
- ¼ teaspoon nutmeg

Preheat oven to 325°F.

Combine juice and honey. Mix in egg yolks.

Pour into individual custard cups. Lightly sprinkle custard with nutmeg.

Place custard cups in a pan of water and bake for about 1 hour. Cool thoroughly at room temperature, then chill.

CHESTNUT STEW

- 1 pound fresh chestnuts
- 1 cup wild carrots, chopped
- ½ cup wild parsnip, chopped
- 1 cup wild greens, cooked
- 1 teaspoon lemon juice
- 1 cup wild celery stalks, chopped
- 1 teaspoon wild caraway seeds
- 1 tablespoon sunflower seeds
- 1 teaspoon marjoram
- 1 quart hot Wild Vegetable Stock (page 77)

Shell chestnuts and slice in half. Place in boiling water and simmer for 20 minutes.

Drain chestnuts. Place in a large kettle.

Add all remaining ingredients with enough Wild Vegetable Stock to cover amply. Bring to a boil over high heat.

Immediately reduce heat and simmer, covered, 40 minutes. Serve with tossed wild salad and Acorn-Rye Muffins (page 301).

Yield: *6 servings*

FRESH-ROASTED PIÑON NUTS

Every year throughout the West, many people willingly travel long distances to visit piñon country where they gather these wonderful nuts. Most people simply spread sheets or blankets under the trees and then shake the branches. A few years ago we visited a coal mine in the front range of the Rockies, where we were able to trade 3 pounds of piñon nuts for 2 tons of good coal.

Preheat oven to 275°F.

Spread a single layer of piñon nuts in a shallow baking sheet. Do not add salt, butter, or oil.

Roast in a slow oven for 30 minutes or until the nuts are oily and obviously roasted.

HEALTHFUL NUT FILLING

- 1 cup wild (*or* domestic) nuts, slivered or ground
- ½ cup dark honey
- 1 teaspoon cinnamon
- 1 tablespoon orange peel, grated
- 1 egg, beaten light
- 3 tablespoons soy milk

In a mixing bowl, combine nuts, honey, cinnamon, and orange peel. Mix thoroughly.

Add well-beaten egg and soy milk. Stir. Spread over coffee cake or pastry dough and bake.

CHAPTER FOURTEEN

WILD DESSERTS

Here we have some fancy desserts that are unusually light and healthful. None of these will sabotage a cook's hard work by overcoming an already hearty and spirited wild dinner. And none of the afternoon desserts, such as Berry-Honey Froth, will ruin your dinner or your day with a ton of undigested sweetness.

Older or bruised fruit may be used in most of the fruit dessert recipes. Fresh, whole fruit should, of course, be used as it comes.

WILD
DESSERTS

PIE CRUST

The following recipe from *The Rodale Cookbook* by Nancy Albright is a standard pie crust recipe that you can use in many ways.

   1 **cup barley flour**

   ½ **cup oat flour**

   ⅓ **cup oil**

   4 **tablespoons ice water**

Preheat oven to 400°F.

Brush bottom and sides of a 9-inch pie tin with oil.

Sift dry ingredients into a bowl. (We sift together twice.)

Mix oil and ice water. (Sounds strange, but it works.)

Add liquid to dry ingredients using a fork. Stir until a ball is formed.

Press into pie tin, or roll between layers of wax paper and place in pie tin.

Prick an appropriate pattern into the crust using a sharp fork. Bake for 10 − 12 minutes.

BERRY COBBLER

- 4 cups ripe serviceberries (*or* mountain ash berries), carefully selected and washed
- 1 teaspoon wild rice flour
- ½ cup light honey
- 1 cup cornmeal
- 1 teaspoon baking powder
- 1 teaspoon coltsfoot ash
- ½ cup sour milk
- 2 tablespoons safflower oil
- 1 cup Wild Berry Sauce (page 338)

Preheat oven to 375°F.

Place berries in a large baking dish. Sprinkle with flour and dot with honey.

In a mixing bowl, combine dry ingredients. Stir in milk and oil.

Drop batter on berries by the tablespoon. Pour on ½ of the Wild Berry Sauce. Bake for 1 hour. Cool and serve with remaining Wild Berry Sauce.

Yield: *6 − 8 servings*

WILD DESSERTS

WILD BERRIES POACHED IN HONEY

This is a traditional recipe widely enjoyed by berry gatherers. It is especially appropriate when your berries are not of the best texture, color, or flavor. Berries that are not quite ripe taste fine when poached in honey.

- ½ cup honey
- ½ cup water
- 3 cups fresh wild berries (wild strawberries are excellent)

Combine honey and water in a pot over medium heat. Bring to a boil, then simmer for 3 or 4 minutes.

With honey mixture at a slow simmer, add berries. Increase heat to bring to second boil. Immediately reduce heat to slow simmer for 5 minutes.

Serve hot over biscuits or refrigerate and serve cold in dessert cups.

Yield: *4 servings*

BAKED WILD APPLES WITH CURRANTS

We have modified this traditional recipe to avoid the use of sugar and butter and to allow for baking at home or on the trail. Few treats are as well known and yet so seldom encountered.

6 – 10	wild apples
½	cup dark honey
1	cup currants (*or* raisins)
1	tablespoon cinnamon
¼	teaspoon nutmeg
½	teaspoon lemon rind, grated
¼	cup safflower oil

Preheat oven to 375°F or reduce campfire to glowing coals.

Wash apples and partially core to create a cuplike cavity. Remove a thin strip of peel from the tops of the apples.

Combine honey, currants, cinnamon, nutmeg, and lemon rind. Mix well and stuff the apples with this mixture.

Brush apples with safflower oil and wrap loosely with aluminum foil.

Place wrapped apples on a baking sheet in the oven or set directly in hot campfire coals. When the foil discolors, the apples are done. Serve hot or cold.

Yield: *6 – 10 servings*

WILD DESSERTS

WILD FRUIT OR BERRY SAUCE

- 2 cups fruit (wild strawberries are best) (*or* whole wild berries)
- 1 cup wild fruit (*or* berry) juice
- ¼ cup honey
- 2½ tablespoons cornstarch
- 1 tablespoon lemon juice

Combine fruit with juice, honey, and cornstarch in a saucepan. Place over medium heat and stir until mixture is clear and thickened, about 30 minutes.

Stir in lemon juice. Continue to cook and stir 3 minutes longer.

Chill thoroughly. Serve as dessert topping, over pancakes, or use in recipes calling for puréed fruit.

WILD APPLESAUCE

It's best to choose a good selection of wild apples that includes a mix of about 50 percent very ripe apples and 50 percent bruised green apples.

- 2 pounds wild apples, washed and cored
- 1 cup light honey
- ½ cup wild berry juice
- 2 cups water

cinnamon (optional)

Do not peel the apples. Cut into thin wedges.

Place all ingredients in a kettle over moderate heat. Bring to a boil, then reduce heat and simmer 1 hour, stirring frequently.

Remove from heat and allow to sit for 10 minutes. Serve hot with cinnamon, or cold.

Yield: *8 servings*

apple

STEAMED BERRY PUDDING

This recipe will work well with almost any wild berry or fruit but is best with the more tart varieties like gooseberry or cranberry.

  ¼ cup butter

1¼ cups honey

  4 eggs, beaten until light

  1 cup wild berries (*or* fruit), sliced

  3 cups flour

  3 teaspoons baking powder

  1 teaspoon coltsfoot ash

Cream butter and honey until smooth.

Stir eggs into creamed butter and add berries.

Sift flour, baking powder, and coltsfoot ash together. Gradually stir into berry mixture.

Grease and dust well with flour a large pudding mold. Fill with pudding mixture and cover tightly.

Place mold in a large pot with enough boiling water to come nearly halfway up the mold. Cover pot and steam gently for 2 hours.

Remove mold to a cold place and chill for 10 minutes. Turn onto a platter and serve.

Yield: *4 — 6 servings*

POND LILY POPCORN

Yes, even popcorn can be replaced by a wild substitute. Gather the pods in late summer and sun-dry them or store them until dry. Then remove the seeds and store them in covered jars at room temperature. While you're gathering the seeds, you may as well collect a sackful of the tubers, which are excellent when baked in a slow oven.

    3   tablespoons corn oil
1 — 2   cups pond lily seeds, dried
    1   teaspoon coltsfoot ash

Place oil in a large, heavy skillet, cold, and add pond lily seeds no more than 1 or 2 deep.

Place cold skillet over high heat. When the seeds begin to open, move the pan as necessary to prevent burning. No need to shake, as with ordinary popcorn.

When all the seeds have popped, remove from heat and pour into a bowl. Sprinkle with coltsfoot ash and serve hot.

Yield: *8 servings*

WILD STRAWBERRIES AND COCONUT

    3 cups wild strawberries

    ¼ cup light honey

    ¼ cup coconut, shredded

Slice strawberries in half and layer in dessert cups, each layer dribbled with honey.

Dribble honey over top layer of berries in each cup. Sprinkle with coconut. Serve well chilled.

Yield: *4 servings*

BERRY SHERBET

    2 cups wild berry juice

    ¼ cup honey

    1 teaspoon lemon juice

    3 teaspoons unflavored gelatin

1½ cups juicy berries, lightly mashed

    2 egg whites

    1 teaspoon violet flowers and buds, minced

Combine berry juice, honey, and lemon juice in a kettle. Place over medium heat and add gelatin, a little at a time, stirring constantly. Do not boil.

When gelatin is dissolved and thoroughly blended, remove from heat and allow to cool. Stir in berries.

Pour sherbet into a shallow dish and place in freezer. Check frequently and remove when almost frozen.

Turn sherbet into a large bowl. Stir in egg whites and violet flowers and buds. Beat until nicely whipped.

Place in freezer for 24 hours. Before serving, use a whisk to whip until frothy. Serve cold and store in freezer.

Yield: *4 servings*

BERRY-HONEY FROTH

Try this method with bruised or overripe berries. It's an attractive and unusual dessert, though very easy to prepare.

- 3 **cups fresh wild berries**
- ½ **cup honey**
- ½ **cup yogurt**
- 1 **tablespoon cold water**
- **yogurt for topping**

Combine berries, honey, yogurt, and water in a blender. Purée until smooth and frothy.

Serve immediately in fancy dessert bowls, topped with yogurt, or chill overnight and blend again briefly before serving.

Yield: *4 servings*

EASY WILD FRUIT PUDDING

½	cup wild rice flour
3	cups wild fruit juice (*or* cider)
1	teaspoon violet flowers and buds, minced
1½	cups wild berries, lightly mashed
½	cup light honey
1	scant tablespoon safflower oil
½	teaspoon spicebush
¼	cup berries

Place flour in a large kettle. Gradually pour in wild fruit juice, blending constantly with a whisk. Add violet flowers and buds.

Place over low heat and bring to a boil, stirring frequently. Reduce heat and simmer until mixture thickens.

Stir in wild berries. Simmer for 5 minutes. Remove from heat and stir in remaining ingredients. Serve hot immediately, or pour into dessert cups and chill overnight.

Yield: *4 servings*

WILD NUT PUDDING

   2 cups wild nuts (walnuts, hazelnuts, *or* chestnuts)

1½ cups yogurt

  ½ cup skim milk

  ¼ cup honey

   3 tablespoons coconut, shredded

  ¼ cup cracked ice

wild mint (optional)

Combine nuts, yogurt, and skim milk in a saucepan. Place over very low heat and cook until nuts are fairly soft, about 40 minutes. Do not boil.

Place nut mixture and all other ingredients in a blender. Purée. Place in individual dessert cups and chill 2 hours before serving. If desired, garnish with wild mint.

Yield: *4 servings*

INDEX

A

Erodium cicutarium. See Heron's bill
Evening primrose, as cooked vegetable, 247–48

F

G

L

M

N

W

Y